FREEDOM OF SPEECH AND EXPRESSION

THE RUTGERS LECTURES IN PHILOSOPHY

Larry Temkin, series editor

RUTGERS
School of Arts and Sciences

Published in the series

Vagueness: A Global Approach
Kit Fine

FREEDOM OF SPEECH
AND EXPRESSION

Its History, Its Value, Its Good Use,
and Its Misuse

Richard Sorabji

OXFORD
UNIVERSITY PRESS

OXFORD

UNIVERSITY PRESS

Oxford University Press is a department of the University of Oxford. It furthers the University's objective of excellence in research, scholarship, and education by publishing worldwide. Oxford is a registered trade mark of Oxford University Press in the UK and certain other countries.

Published in the United States of America by Oxford University Press 198 Madison Avenue, New York, NY 10016, United States of America.

© Oxford University Press 2021

Library of Congress Cataloging-in-Publication Data
Names: Sorabji, Richard, author.
Title: Freedom of speech and expression : its history, its value, its good use, and its misuse / Richard Sorabji.
Description: New York, NY : Oxford University Press, 2021. | Includes bibliographical references and index.
Identifiers: LCCN 2020037508 (print) | LCCN 2020037509 (ebook) | ISBN 9780197532157 (hardback) | ISBN 9780197532171 (epub)
Subjects: LCSH: Freedom of speech. | Freedom of expression. | Social media.
Classification: LCC JC591.S66 2021 (print) | LCC JC591 (ebook) | DDC 323.44/3—dc23
LC record available at https://lccn.loc.gov/2020037508
LC ebook record available at https://lccn.loc.gov/2020037509

DOI: 10.1093/oso/9780197532157.001.0001

1 3 5 7 9 8 6 4 2

Printed by Integrated Books International, United States of America

"Cicero denouncing Catiline" by John Leech. Courtesy of the Posner Memorial Collection, Special Collections, Carnegie Mellon University Libraries, Pittsburgh PA. From Gilbert Abbott A. Beckett and John Leech, *The Comic History of Rome*. London 1870: Bradbury, Evans & Co. (DG210 A12 1852A).

To Laila and Nadia

CONTENTS

SERIES EDITOR FOREWORD

In 2014, I had the distinct privilege of being Chair of the Department of Philosophy at Rutgers, The State University of New Jersey. Soon after I become Chair, Peter Ohlin, philosophy editor of Oxford University Press, USA, broached the idea of Rutgers organizing a major annual lecture series, where Rutgers would carefully select among the world's leading philosophers to give a series of three original lectures which would be subsequently revised for publication in a book series by Oxford University Press. It was Peter's hope that such a series might soon come to be recognized as one of the most important annual events on the philosophical calendar, and might one day come to rival the Locke Lectures, Dewey Lectures, and Tanner Lectures in stature.

I shared Peter's enthusiasm for the idea, and promised to take it up with my colleagues and our administration. Unsurprisingly, the response was overwhelmingly supportive. However, it was decided that if we were going to take on such a commitment, we wanted the endeavour to involve much more than just adding another three lectures, each year, to our already crowded academic calendar. We wanted to create a lecture series that was truly distinctive and special; one that would benefit not only our faculty, but our outstanding graduate students, undergraduates, and the wider Rutgers community. Moreover, we were especially concerned to create a lecture series that would be both personally and intellectually rewarding for our visiting speakers.

After much discussion, the *Rutgers Lectures in Philosophy* took shape. First, the Department was committed to bringing in genuinely world-class philosophers who had already done, and were continuing to do, seminal work that was profoundly impacting their areas of research and, in some cases, the world at large. Our hope, and expectation, was that the lectures they would be delivering at Rutgers, and the books based on those lectures, would help set the philosophical agendas in their respective fields for many years to come. Bearing that goal foremost in mind, we were also committed to inviting a diverse group of speakers, representing a broad spectrum of philosophical areas and interests within the analytic tradition.

Second, speakers would be asked to be available on campus for a full week, and to pitch their first lecture so that interested alumni, the broader Rutgers academic community, and the general public might benefit from these internationally renowned philosophers. Their two subsequent lectures would be aimed at the high philosophical level that would most benefit the Philosophy faculty, graduate students, visitors, and speaker, and would likely form the backbone of the speaker's subsequent book. Each lecture would be followed by discussion, a reception, and dinner, to facilitate serious engagement with the speaker's views.

Third, speakers would distribute drafts of their lectures, which would be read and discussed in advance by interested faculty, graduate students, and visitors. Then, there would be an intensive workshop with the speaker on the distributed material during their week on campus, providing the speaker with valuable feedback, and the workshop members with the chance to get to know the speaker and his or her views in a seminar setting.

Fourth, there would be a separate lunch meeting with the speaker for interested undergraduate majors, minors, philosophy club members, and students working on the undergraduate philosophy journal, *Arete*. As it turns out, several speakers have reported their meeting with our undergraduates to be one of the biggest highlights of their visits!

Finally, speakers would be encouraged to hang around the Department for impromptu discussions, and to set up individual meetings with faculty or graduate students particularly interested in their work.

A little over two years after Peter Ohlin and I first spoke, the first *Rutgers Lectures in Philosophy* took place, and at this point the first four lectures in the Series have been delivered. The first book in the series, Kit Fine's *Vagueness: A Global Approach* has been published, and now this, the second book in the series, will appear. It has been a long road between Peter Ohlin's original idea and this moment, but we couldn't be more pleased by how the lecture and book series have developed. It has truly been everything we envisaged it to be and more.

There are many people I would like to thank for helping to make the *Rutgers Lectures in Philosophy* possible. I apologize, in advance, for the fact that nothing I say here can remotely reflect the depth of my gratitude to those who have worked tirelessly behind the scenes to make this series a success. I also apologize to anyone I inadvertently forget to mention. On both scores, please forgive me.

First, my deep gratitude to Peter Ohlin, who not only planted the seed from which this lecture and book series has grown, but who has helped to nurture it and bring it to fruition at every step of the way. Peter's contributions to this series have been both invaluable and indispensable. My thanks, also, to Peter's excellent team at OUP, from the Editorial Board, to copyeditors, design artists, publicists, production managers, and so on, all of whom do yeomen's work in bringing a book to press, and making sure that it receives the attention it deserves. Thanks, also, to Peter Momtchiloff, Oxford University Press's philosophy editor in the United Kingdom, for sage advice in this project's initial stages. And a special thanks to the referees for the volumes in this series, whose conscientious work are almost always underappreciated by everyone but the authors.

In the Department of Philosophy, my biggest debt is to my colleagues, who were extremely supportive of this project from the get go, and who have spent countless hours deliberating about the Series format and possible speakers, and attending the numerous series events. I also want to thank all the graduate students who have actively participated in Series events, with a special thanks to Jimmy Goodrich and Adam Gibbons, who have done much of the heavy organizational lifting. I also owe a debt of gratitude to two business managers, Pauline Mitchell and Charlene Jones, our undergraduate administrative assistants, Jean Urteil and Jessica Koza, and, especially, our graduate administrative assistant, Mercedes Diaz, for all their hard work. Justin Kalef has organized the undergraduate luncheon meetings, and I am grateful to him, and all the undergraduates who have made that event a highlight of the lecture series. Special thanks is also owed to Dean Zimmerman, current Chair of the Rutgers Philosophy Department, for his crucial and unwavering support.

This series would never exist were it not for the substantial support that the Philosophy Department has received over many years from the Rutgers Administration, including Presidents, Chancellors, Vice-Presidents, and Deans. The *Rutgers Lectures in Philosophy* series thrives because of the incredibly vibrant and congenial philosophical environment that the Rutgers

Administration has made possible. I, and my colleagues, can't thank them enough. I can't possibly name every important administrator whose support has helped make the Rutgers Philosophy Department what it is today, but I need to mention a few: first and foremost, the current President, Robert Barchi. President Barchi is committed to excellence, and has been a great champion of our department. Following the President's lead, Chancellor Richard Edwards and current Chancellor Christopher Malloy have both been enormously supportive.

A number of people in the Dean's office have worked very hard, and successfully, to give the Rutgers Lectures in Philosophy Series a high profile not only *within* Rutgers, but *globally*. These include Kara Donaldson, who oversaw these efforts, Ian DeFalco, and John Chadwick. James Masschaele, Vice Dean of the School of Arts and Sciences, has been supportive from its onset, and Michelle Stephens has been supportive since becoming Dean of Humanities. Two people are deserving of special mention: James Swenson, former Dean of Humanities, and currently Vice Provost for Academic Affairs, and Peter March, Executive Dean of the School of Arts and Sciences. To each, my heartfelt thanks for all they have done over many years to support the Philosophy Department in general, and the Lecture Series in particular.

Finally, my biggest thanks go to the stars of the Series, the speakers whose path-breaking work is an inspiration to all those in the field. I am most grateful to those who helped put the series on the philosophical map, by agreeing to be one of our distinguished speakers. As of now, the lineup of speakers is: Kit Fine (2016), Sir Richard Sorabji (2017), Robert Stalnaker (2018), Jeff McMahan (2019), Béatrice Longuenesse (2020), Tim Williamson (2021), Philip Kitcher (2022), and Susanna Siegel (2023).

Sir Richard Sorabji was and is everything we were seeking in a speaker. He presented entirely new work on a topic of fundamental importance socially, politically, and morally. Throughout his visit he was lively, modest, engaging, and accessible to all. And since his visit he has been both eager and diligent about revising and improving his book in a timely manner. He has truly been an exemplary scholar in every respect throughout this process, and an editor's dream. The book you are now reading, *Freedom of Speech and Expression: Its History, Its Value, Its Good Use, and Its Misuse*, is certain to be a rich source of inspiration and discussion for years to come. I am extremely pleased to have Sir Richard's book appear as the second book in the Rutgers Lectures in Philosophy Series. Those of us associated with the series have hoped that one day it would be widely recognized for its philosophical excellence. I have no doubt that Sir Richard's book is another important step towards the realization of that hope.

Again, to everyone who has helped in bringing this book to press, and most especially Sir Richard Sorabji, my heartfelt gratitude.

Larry S. Temkin, Series Editor
New Brunswick, New Jersey
April 2020

ACKNOWLEDGEMENTS

I was very pleased to be invited in 2016 by Professor Larry Temkin, on behalf of the Rutgers University Philosophy Department in partnership with the Oxford University Press, to deliver the 2017 Rutgers Lectures in Philosophy. The third Rutgers lecture has been replaced by a new chapter in order to address a major contemporary problem—social media.

I have benefitted from many discussions and written works, which I have tried to acknowledge in the main text. But here I should like to pick out two particular kinds of help.

The first was the highly valuable discussions during my week of lecturing at Rutgers University in October and November of 2017. The second was the detailed, closely considered, and clarifying comments obtained for me by Oxford University

Press, New York, on the penultimate draft of this book. One set was from my colleague in Oxford, Professor Jeff McMahan, who is himself the author of the 2019 lectures at the Rutgers Philosophy Department, his former base. The other was from Professor Han Baltussen at the Philosophy Department of the University of Adelaide, who led me to revise the structure of the book. I am grateful to Jane Potter for introducing me to the idea of citizen journalists.

I am grateful also to my friend and colleague Professor William Twining for giving me a jurisprudential view on chapter 3, and to the Oxford University Press editor in New York, Peter Ohlin, for very helpful comments on chapters 1 and 3. I also gained valuable comments, queries, and reading suggestions from an anonymous review commissioned by David Schmidtz, editor of *Social Policy and Philosophy*, in return for writing a version of chapter 3, without its appendix, for that journal. For me, writing good philosophy depends on such opportunities for discussion and comment.

Richard Sorabji

INTRODUCTION

I encountered the denial of free speech twice, once in my early days, when I was taught Russian by charming emigrés from Stalin's Soviet Union, all of whom had terrifying tales to tell of unfreedom. I encountered it again, when I went behind the Iron Curtain to Prague in Czechoslovakia to talk about Aristotle's *Metaphysics* with a group of academics, who had been sacked from the university and turned into window cleaners by a Soviet-dominated government so ignorant that it believed Aristotle's *Metaphysics* might be politically dangerous. We met in private houses after working hours, could not speak each other's names aloud, because the walls were bugged, and when my hosts wanted to continue discussion after midnight, they

Freedom of Speech and Expression. Richard Sorabji, Oxford University Press (2021). © Oxford University Press. DOI: 10.1093/oso/9780197532157.001.0001

could not come to my hotel for fear of incriminating the person who had separately booked me in, so we had to stand outside in the snow, in order to continue talking about Aristotle. I had to memorise, not write down, the titles of scholarly books they would like me to send them from England, and after the one member of the group still allowed to teach in Prague was also allowed to visit London University for three months of research, he committed suicide rather than return.

In 2012, I published a book on Mahatma Gandhi and the all-important philosophy of non-violence, compassion for opponents, and voluntary suffering, which led eventually to the end of British rule in India and I compared aspects of that philosophy with ancient Stoicism.[1] I was particularly impressed by Gandhi's conception of *opening ears*. He sought to open ears not by propaganda to the masses, but by non-violent *satyagraha*: insistence on truth both to himself and to his powerful opponents, the British rulers of India. At least two British Viceroys felt some admiration for him, and eventually, he opened the ears of world opinion. These experiences of discussion and reading are part of what lay behind my interest in the subject of freedom of speech and expression, its history and its right use.

In this volume, chapter 1 points out that the idea of free speech for all became widespread comparatively late. On

1. Richard Sorabji, *Gandhi and the Stoics, Modern Experiments on Ancient Values*, Oxford University Press, Oxford, and the University of Chicago Press, Chicago, 2012.

the whole, it was treated as a prerogative of some people only, although an early exception was the Buddhist emperor Ashoka in India, who encouraged Buddhists of all persuasions to live and talk with each other and learn from each other, and people of different religions to do the same. Although it otherwise took a long time for free speech and expression to be extended to all, nonetheless, through different ages and cultures from antiquity to the present, the award of free speech, whether to some or to all, was seen as resulting in speech of a beneficial sort. That is why my title speaks of *good* speech and its misuse, rather than simply of speech and its misuse.

Chapter 2 argues that John Stuart Mill supported free speech on the grounds of the beneficial effects it can have, in Chapter 2 of his *On Liberty* of 1859. But the history in chapter 1 suggests that this has been a recurrent view through the ages. If free speech is valued for its benefits, speech that frustrates those benefits suggests a clear boundary on free speech which should appeal voluntarily to its supporters. Their voluntary self-restraint in speech should normally be better than legal constraint for keeping speech beneficial. But self-restraint is not the only preserver of benefits. Speech that opens ears, to take an expression of Gandhi's, in his case the ears of powerful opponents, is also a preserver of benefits.

Chapter 3 turns to an important problem of our time. It says that law is after all required if we are to preserve our freedoms, when some of the online social media offset the benefits they have to offer by basing their profits on exploiting personal profiles based on personal data left online by users. It spells out the bad effects of this and counters the suggestion that any media producing these bad effects can claim to be supporting free speech as understood by those reviewed in chapters 1 and 2. It supports the education of nine- to eleven-year-olds in detecting fake news and targeted news, and recommends encouraging compliant media. But with reference to Government documents, it also proposes new legislation and new methods of enforcement against such misuse of speech.

FREEDOM OF SPEECH AND EXPRESSION

Chapter 1

The benefits seen in free speech and its gradual extension from some to all

An intercultural history

The idea of free speech for all became widespread comparatively late, we shall see. On the whole, it was treated as a prerogative of elites, although an early exception of a kind was the ancient Buddhist emperor Ashoka in India, who encouraged people of all religious groups to live and talk with each other and learn from each other. But even Ashoka was talking about all religious *groups*, not about all individuals. Free speech was not for all individuals, and it still has other kinds of legal constraint: people cannot say whatever they like. Moreover, from antiquity, people treated the need for beneficial speech as a

Freedom of Speech and Expression. Richard Sorabji, Oxford University Press (2021). © Oxford University Press. DOI: 10.1093/oso/9780197532157.003.0001

reason for, and constraint on, free speech. I shall cite examples of both.

1.2. THE NEED FOR FREEDOM OF EXPRESSION AND SPEECH

As we can see it nowadays, freedom of speech for everyone was an enormous gift, won by great bravery at the cost of personal danger, and for purposes of political, religious, and social freedom.[1] It is important to recognize how damaging it can be when this freedom is denied. I will start with the *negative* case for freedom of speech—the damage caused by its suppression. This supports the idea of free speech as a right. But I shall discuss later the positive benefits envisaged by its advocates, which present it as a social good, whether or not it is also pursued as a right.

One outstanding example of the negative case has been given by Timothy Garton Ash in his book, *The File,*[2] from his experience under the Stasi in East Germany, where even a wife found that her husband was reporting on the family's daily activities to the secret police. When the regime had fallen, Garton Ash demanded to see the file kept on him, with the names of the ordinary people informing on his

---

1. Speech itself involves expression, but in some cases discussed in a later chapter, such as cartooning, the expression does not take the form of speech in the strictest sense. I shall sometimes, however, for brevity refer to expression as speech even in these contexts.
2. Timothy Garton Ash, *The File*, Random House, New York, 1997.

movements, meetings, and words, and confronted them to ask why they had informed. My own brief experience in the former Czechoslovakia, though negligible by comparison, was quite unpleasant enough. I was one of many who responded to an organization arranging visits to Prague, to help a group of academics sacked from the university and forbidden to read Aristotle, in case he was dangerous. Some of the academics had been turned into window-cleaners. They wanted to meet in secret in their homes at night to study Aristotle's *Metaphysics*, in which the only semi-political remark compares God with the general who gives unity to an army. My first mistake in two private homes was to ask our host's name. The silence was broken by the host, who said he could tell his name because his walls were bugged with listening devices anyhow, and his name would be known, but the names of the others should not be spoken. When in the second home they wanted to continue discussing the *Metaphysics* after midnight, they could not come to talk in my hotel, in case the person who booked me in could be identified with the dissident readers of Aristotle, and we had to stand talking in the snow outside. When they asked me to send more up-to-date texts of Aristotle and books about him from the United Kingdom, they stopped me writing down the titles and asked me to memorize the list instead, in case I was interrogated at the airport. Most of them were not allowed to use the university library. The one who did retain a ticket to read about ancient Greek civilization was refused a book on Greek astronomy because astronomy was not on his ticket. That man was later allowed to accept a colleague's invitation to visit London University for three months, but he committed suicide rather than return.

At a still later conference in West Berlin, I tried to pass through the wall to East Berlin for an afternoon visit to the museums, with a colleague who had had a far more frightening visit to Prague, having been arrested and driven at night to exit the border on foot in the headlights of the vehicle. He had not realized that his passport had been marked in such a way as to exclude him from other Communist countries too, and he could not follow me through the barrier, so that we both lost our afternoon visit. These small experiences, and others, left me in no doubt about the importance of free speech.

1.2. ASHOKA, INDIAN EMPEROR, THIRD CENTURY BCE: FREE SPEECH FOR ALL RELIGIOUS AFFILIATIONS, BUT WITH BOUNDARIES TO SECURE THE BENEFITS

The idea of freedom of speech for all religious affiliations is found in Rock Edict VII of the emperor Ashoka, inscribed on rock in the third century BCE, to which recent work by Rajeev Bhargava has drawn my attention.[3] Already, long before any

---

3. I draw here on Rajeev Bhargava, 'Beyond toleration: civility and principled coexistence in Ashokan edicts', in Alfred Stepan and Charles Taylor, eds., *Boundaries of*

such universal concept existed in Europe, the emperor Ashoka, having converted to Buddhism, desired freedom of speech for everyone. His inscriptions do not say for all individuals, but for all the *pasandas*, or religious affiliations. In his Edict VII, Romila Thapar tells me, he was thinking of different affiliations within Buddhism. He encouraged all affiliations to be admitted to live everywhere. He did not want rival affiliations shut out. In Edict XII, he moved from free speech to beneficial speech. Referring to all religions in his vast Indian kingdom, he desired them through harmony (*samovaya*) to learn, respect, and know the doctrines of other affiliations, and to acquire sound doctrines. If he meant that that is how to learn sound doctrines, he would be anticipating J. S. Mill's extrapolation from the Roman lawyer Cicero, who said from the different context of legal dispute, that he studied his opponent's case with as great or greater intensity than his own. Mill's conclusion is that you don't know your own case until you know that of your opponent. On another translation, Romila Thapar tells me, Ashoka required more than *knowledge* of the doctrines of others, and said instead that affiliations should learn, respect, and *listen to* the doctrines of others. Ashoka also set a boundary. He desired restraint on speech (*vacaguti*) such as has not yet even now been widely accepted in the West for relations between communities. He desires them all to avoid disparagement of other religious affiliations, or over-glorification of

Toleration, Columbia University Press, New York, 2014, pp. 173–202, and subsequent discussion with Romila Thapar.

their own.[4] Others can be criticized, but not without reason and not immoderately. Moreover, the inscriptions prudently present these not as law, but as the powerful emperor's desires. The medium for learning the beliefs of others will have been not only speech, but *discussion*, to which Mill, in another age, would also attach so much importance, and the emperor's appeal to his desires, rather than his commands, shows that he valued the tone in which his message was expressed. In other cases in this book, I shall sometimes discuss expression which does not take the form of speech, but here the expression is concerned with speech and writing.

Admittedly, those who could read his inscriptions might be cautioned by the former brutality with which, before his conversion to Buddhism, he conquered the only kingdom of comparable strength in India, that of the people slightly to the south of his and on the east coast, where modern Odisha (formerly Orissa) is now. But he does acknowledge this and express apparently genuine 'remorse' for the brutality of this conquest in his Rock Edict XIII. As described in the book on political violence by Upinder Singh,[5] this edict addresses a wider range of people, including those who live in the forests, as opposed to farmers or dwellers in settlements. The forest-dwellers were

---

4. Ashoka's constraint on over-glorification is a refinement not represented, for example, in the clause included at Christian insistence in the constitution of India after 1947 of the right to promulgate one's own religion.

5. Upinder Singh, *Political Violence in Ancient India*, Harvard University Press, Cambridge MA, 2017, pp. 268–271; 387–389.

more dependent for their food on killing animals.[6] Moreover, their interests were opposed to the encroachment of farmers into the forests, and to the greater wealth of the settlements outside both forests and farms. The edict proclaims, 'Even the forest people he conciliates and urges to reflect. And they are told of the power that [he] has in spite of his remorse, so that they may turn away from their crimes and not be killed. For [he] desires for all beings freedom from injury, self-restraint, impartiality and kindness'. There is a threat here, at least to the people whom it was hardest to control.

To return to the edicts seeking reconciliation among different persuasions in Buddhism, Bhargava quotes Rock Edict XII in the translation of N. A. Nikam and Richard McKeon, *The Edicts of Asoka*. This explains part of the *Dhamma* (Prakrit for *Dharma*) that he enjoins, roughly moral duty:

The faiths of others all deserve to be honoured for one reason or another. By honouring them, one exalts one's own faith and at the same time performs a service to the faith of others. By acting otherwise, one injures one's own faith and also does disservice to that of others. For if a man extols his own faith and disparages another because of devotion to his own and because he wants to glorify it, he seriously injures his own faith.

---

6. For protection of animals, Upinder Singh cites, pp. 392–398: Rock Edicts I, II, IV, VIII, IX, and XI, and Pillar Edict V.

Therefore concord alone is commendable, for through concord men may learn and respect the concept of Dharma accepted by others. King Priyadarsi[7] desires men of all faiths to know[8] each other's doctrines and to acquire sound doctrines.

1.3. FREE SPEECH APPROVED BY ATHENS FOR COMIC POETS, CITIZENS OF THE DEMOCRACY, ATHENIAN CYNIC PHILOSOPHERS

I have not found freedom of speech or expression being claimed for *everyone*, at least in Europe, before the seventeenth century. Aristotle thought that brothers should grant free speech to brothers and to comrades.[9] In Shakespeare only the court jester is granted free speech. So in India is the king's joker, or *vidushaka*, in the performance of certain ancient Sanskrit plays.[10] Similarly in ancient Greece, comic poets were among the few to whom free speech was allowed. Alan Sommerstein

---

7. Or 'Piyadassi', explained by Romila Thapar, *Aśoka and the Decline of the Mauryas*, Oxford University Press, Delhi, paperback edition 1998, p. 349, as a name assumed by Ashoka meaning 'of gracious mien'. The first decipherer of the inscriptions, Prinsep, was not at first aware (p. 7) that the name referred to Ashoka.

8. The translation 'know' is also given by Romila Thapar, in her *Aśoka and the Decline of the Mauryas*, Rock Edicts, p. 382, even though she considers 'listen to' a possible alternative.

9. Aristotle, *Nicomachean Ethics*, 9.2, 1165a29–30.

10. Sudha Gopalakrishnan, Kutyattam, *The Heritage Theatre of India*, Nyogi Books, New Delhi, 2011, pp. 47, 120.

has discussed how the populist politician Cleon brought, or tried to bring, the leading comic poet, Aristophanes, to court, possibly twice.[11] But he failed to have him silenced, and in play after play was mercilessly satirized by Aristophanes, including for his efforts to use the law. A contemporary of Aristophanes, 'The Old Oligarch' is cited, in a work wrongly ascribed to Xenophon, as saying that the Athenians allowed satire in comedy on rich, well-born, or powerful individuals, but did not allow it on the citizenry in general. This may relate to a scholium on Aristophanes's play, *Acharnians*, Line 67, reporting that a 'decree about not satirising in comedy' was repealed after three years in 440–439 BCE. If there was such a decree, it will have been short-lived and will not have spared the prominent.[12]

Free speech (not *parrhēsia*—saying everything, or frank speech—but *equal* speech, *isēgoria*) was given its widest extent when granted in the one city of Athens, during its democratic period, to all adult male Athenian citizens present in the democratic Assembly, which they were expected to attend. It looks as if advice from qualified citizens was considered too valuable to be inhibited in democratic decision-making. At least free speech was granted them provided they and their citizen parents were not guilty of disgraceful conduct.[13] So respectability

---

11. Alan H. Sommerstein, 'Harassing the Satirist: The alleged attempts to prosecute Aristophanes', in I. Sluiter and R. M. Rosen, eds., *Free Speech in Classical Antiquity*, Mnemosyne Supplement 254, Brill, Leiden, 2004, pp. 145–174.
12. Ps-Xenophon, *The Constitution of Athens*, 2.18, and scholium to Aristophanes *Acharnians*, line 67, cited by Sommerstein, 'Harassing the Satirist', at pp. 154–158.
13. Euripides, *Ion* 670–675, and *Hippolytus* 420–425, and Aeschines *Against Timarchus* 1.175, cited by Sommerstein, 'Harassing the Satirist'; the first two by

was required as well. This last requirement imposed a bound-ary within the boundary of citizenship, and we shall see that boundaries within boundaries were quite common in the history of free speech. But the outer boundary of citizenship left undetermined the availability of free speech to a much larger population of women, children, resident foreigners (like Aristotle), and slaves. They had to find out what they could get away with. Moreover, the concession of free speech to citizens in good standing was anyhow disliked by those Athenians who favoured oligarchy.[14]

The Cynics in Athens in the fourth century BCE, whose name associates them with dogs rather than humans, criticized convention and set themselves to follow nature. Accordingly, they practised freedom of speech and expression.[15] Diogenes is said to have lived in a wine jar, eschewing a house, and when asked by his admiring visitor Alexander the Great what gift he would like, is said to have replied, 'stand out of my light'. Nature gave him all he wanted; the conqueror of the known world could add nothing. A story about his pupil, Crates, is that

Michel Foucault, *Fearless Speech*, Semiotext(e), Los Angeles, 2001, ed. Joseph Pearson from lectures at Berkeley, October–November 1983, 'Discourse and truth: The problematization of parrhesia', pp. 30, 34.

14. Foucault, *Fearless Speech*. See also David Konstan, '*Parrhēsia*: Ancient philoso-phy in opposition', in Albert A. Anderson, Steven V. Hicks, and Lech Witkovski, eds., *Mythos and Logos*, Rodopi, 2004, Ch. 3; *Id.* 'Two faces of *parrhēsia*: Free speech and self-expression in ancient Greece', *Antichthon* 46, 2012, pp. 1–13; Peter Brown, *Power and Persuasion in Late Antiquity*, University of Wisconsin Press, Madison, 1992, 'Parrhēsia: The philosopher', pp. 61–70.

15. Diogenes Laertius, *Lives of Eminent Philosophers*, 6.69, on Diogenes's free speech; 6.78 on the marble statue erected to him.

he consummated his marriage to a fellow Cynic in public. This was an expressive act, not a speech-act, but it was an expression of belief. Diogenes violated convention far more outrageously than Socrates, but, so far from sharing his fate, was admired,[16] and it is said that a statue was erected to him of a dog in the best quality Parian marble. The Cynics' rigorous pursuit of a simpler life and criticism of conventional indulgence was valued, even though self-respecting Athenians would not dream of living the same way. It was left to the Stoic school to convert Cynicism into a philosophy that could respectably be joined.

1.4. FREE SPEECH CLAIMED BY OTHER GREEK AND ROMAN PHILOSOPHERS TO PRESERVE THEIR OWN IDEALS IN THE TEETH OF OPPOSITION

The case of Socrates in Athens was very different, even though the Cynic philosophers were later seen as his followers. His free speech led to a charge of corrupting the youth (by asking them ethical questions) and introducing new gods (by appealing to his divine guardian spirit) and he was executed in 399 BCE, even after the restoration of democracy in Athens. Nonetheless, Plato's *Apology*, or *Defence*, describing Socrates's defence at his

---

16. As to why, see Han Baltussen, 'A bark worse than his bite? Diogenes the Cynic and the politics of tolerance in Athens', in Han Baltussen and Peter J. Davis, eds., *The Art of Veiled Speech*, University of Pennsylvania Press, Philadelphia, 2015, pp. 74–93.

trial, portrays him as making a most explicit requirement of freedom for his own kind of speech—interrogating the young about moral character. If the Athenians let him off, on condition of stopping interrogation of the young, he would refuse, because God commanded it, and his obedience to God conferred the greatest ever good on the citizens of Athens (*Apology* 29C–30B). Found guilty, but with the right to propose an alternative to the death penalty, he is presented as repeating that he would, for the same reasons, refuse if invited to leave Athens in silence and keeping quiet (*sigōn, hesukhian agōn, Apology* 37C–E).

When the ancient Roman Republic was being undermined, soon to be replaced by the subsequent empire, it was the Stoic philosophers who were particularly associated with outspoken opposition. Their practice of free speech was forbidden and they spoke at their own risk in order to maintain their ideals in the face of tyranny. Once again their free speech was exercised to preserve a greater good. The Stoic, Cato the Younger, was about to be forcibly dragged at Julius Caesar's behest out of the Republican Senate. But he gave himself up willingly and was followed by others, so that Julius Caesar halted his consultation of the Senate and said he would bypass them and put his proposal straight to the people.[17] With senators in Rome robbed of power under the subsequent emperors in the first century CE, but expected to approve the emperor's decisions,

---

17. Cassius Dio, *Roman History* 38.3, a sadly recurring temptation for rulers, but not always successful.

the Stoic Thrasea Paetus, biographer of Cato, stopped attending the Senate under the tyrannical Nero, and his accusers included the fact of his Stoicism as one of the criminal charges against him,[18] before his deliberate suicide. His son-in-law, the Stoic Helvidius Priscus, is said to have insisted to the emperor that as a Senator he must attend the Senate and give his opinion contrary to the emperor's, even if the emperor killed him,[19] as indeed Vespasian went on to do.

1.5. GOOD AND BAD FREE SPEECH DISTINGUISHED IN THE FOURTH CENTURY CE FOR GREEK CYNIC PHILOSOPHERS

In the fourth century CE, moral restrictions were proposed on Cynic free speech, as seen in the works of two non-Cynics, the Greek philosopher Themistius (active late 340s–384/5 CE), and his imperial pupil, the emperor Julian, in what was by then an imperial capital, Constantinople.[20] Themistius is now best known as a leading author of philosophical commentaries on Aristotle. But in his other roles as a non-Christian in an empire increasingly Christian, he was also an orator and leading civil servant to six emperors, and he felt more at home with

18. Tacitus, *Annals*, 16.22.
19. Epictetus, *Discourses* 1.2.19–21.
20. Further details in the introduction to Richard Sorabji, ed., *Aristotle Reinterpreted*, Bloomsbury, London, 2016.

the five who were Christian than with the one pagan emperor. He insisted against opposition that he must be free to promulgate the ethics of Plato and Aristotle in his role as civil servant, and not only in the privacy of his philosophical school.[21] He claimed also to have exercised free speech, *parrhēsia*, with one of his Christian emperors, apparently the fifth, Valens, despite that emperor's not having an easy manner.[22] We further know that he persuaded Valens to commute the death sentence, not on fellow pagans, but on Christians who were briefly held heretical for supporting the Nicene Creed. Here he is said to have used the argument that God willed there to be different opinions concerning him to enhance reverence because of the difficulty of knowing him.[23]

But Themistius got into difficulties with his pupil the emperor Julian, known as the Apostate from his effort to turn the empire back as far as possible from Christianity to pagan worship. Themistius wrote a lost encomium for Julian, in 355, before he became emperor. He seems to have pictured him as a future philosopher-king and man of action, who would quit indoor life in favour of Herculean deeds in the public arena. But he was rebuffed in a letter from Julian probably of 355, preserved in Arabic translation.[24] Julian cites Plato and Plato's pupil

---

21. Themistius, *Oration* 26, 313; 320–321; 327–328.
22. Themistius, *Oration* 34, 13–14.
23. Socrates scholasticus (Byzantine Church historian), *Ecclesiastical History* 4.32. 2–4.
24. Julian Letter to Themistius, 5–9 and 10, translated by Simon Swain, in *Themistius, Julian and Greek Political Theory under Rome*, Cambridge University Press, Cambridge, 2013. For Alberto Rigolio see the following.

Aristotle ('just to prove I do not completely neglect his works'), the latter against Plato's conception of the philosopher-king—surely a harkening back to some former criticism by the teacher of the pupil for neglecting Aristotle. Plato, Julian replied, had said in the *Laws*,[25] a work which Themistius had taught him, that humans cannot be trusted to carry out such deeds, and that something superhuman, a *daimōn*, would be required to rule over men. As for Aristotle, he agreed with Plato that kings cannot be trusted. The happy life which Aristotle ascribed to the philosopher consisted in activity of a very different sort, not in Herculean physical deeds. The architects of action in Aristotle's *Politics* 1325b 22–23 are acting by their *thoughts*. And (as Julian could have read in Plutarch),[26] Aristotle claimed the right to be as proud of his work on theology as was the conqueror Alexander the Great of his own feats. In the reference to theology, Julian already hints that as philosopher-king he will be confining his interest to religion.

It may have taken some time for Themistius to get an opportunity to mend fences with Julian. He was to write a work, *On Virtue*, lost in Greek, but preserved in Syriac, and now translated by Alberto Rigolio, and published in 2018.[27] Rigolio sees this work as being written in 362 CE, as a response to Julian's *Oration 7 Against Heracleios the Cynic*. Julian, now already emperor, objected to the misuse of free speech by

---

25. Plato *Laws* 713C–714A.
26. Plutarch, *On Progress in Virtue* 78d.
27. Themistius, *On Virtue*, sections 48–53, translated by Alberto Rigolio in the series Ancient Commentators on Aristotle, Bloomsbury Academic, London, 2018.

certain Cynics. The Cynic Heracleios had satirized Julian, and Julian replied that the true Cynic *earns* the right to free speech by a good, devout, and helpful life, as did the first two Cynics. Rigolio takes this to give Themistius the opportunity in his *On Virtue* to support Julian's praise of the right kind of Cynic. But first Themistius has in sections 1–9 to explain that there are several roads in Philosophy leading to the same destination, and then in section 10 to explain why he is praising one road (the Cynic), when he himself takes another (Aristotle's), and had never shown any interest in Cynicism. His support for the Cynic road is given in *On Virtue* 48–53. The true Cynic conceals his admonitions within a pleasant jest. But before criticizing anyone, he asks himself first, 'But am I too one such?', a question also recommended by the Stoic Seneca, to control one's anger.[28] For the Cynic is humble—an idea better known as a Christian virtue. But the Cynic will adjust his humility or severity to the character of the person he is correcting, very much like the teachers in the Epicurean school to be described in chapter 2. As with the Epicureans, though the true Cynic has freedom of speech, there are moral boundaries to that freedom. By following such methods, Diogenes's Cynic pupil Crates left concord behind him in people's houses. (Themistius 53, here uses the same example as Julian 201B–C). Freedom of speech for Cynics was seen as providing a *benefit* to society.

---

28. Seneca, *On Anger* 2.28.

Julian writes again in his *Oration 6, Against the Uneducated Cynics*, which, despite its number, Rigolio places later than *Oration 7* in the same year, 362 CE. There Julian tells a story which well illustrates his view of the true Cynic.[29] Diogenes rebuked a youth who thought the way to start being a Cynic was to make a rude noise in public. Diogenes hit him with his staff, and said that before you violate the conventions of the multitude, you must *earn* the right by subduing your own pleasures and passions.

Further, Julian adds, like his teacher Themistius, the idea that there are *many* roads in Philosophy, although Philosophy is a single thing. This is different from Julian's earlier distinction, in *Against the Cynic Heracleios*, between that Cynic's supposed short cut full of difficulties and the true short cut of using the divine thoughts within oneself, which one can learn by first taking the long way round, as Julian had.[30] Now in the later work, Julian comes closer to Themistius's point about Philosophy's many roads, although he restricts this concession to the best philosophers in each school, thus still excluding the wrong sort of Cynics. The concession has been seen by Rigolio as a nod to Themistius in his *On Virtue* for the idea of many roads in Philosophy. I will, with Rigolio's permission, cite his translation of Themistius on the true Cynic in *On Virtue*, sections 48–53.[31]

---

29. Julian, *Oration 6*, 197B–D.
30. Julian, *Or. 7, Against the Cynic Heracleios* 225C–D, 230C–D, 235C–D.
31. Page and line numbers of Sachau's edition are in square brackets.

48. But if the circumstances demand that the philosopher should say a word of derision while making an accusation, he shall not take pains about how to ridicule so much as how to help, by concealing an admonition under a word of jest, as with the words of Diogenes, in the depths of which [42.5] aid lay hidden beneath the cover of a jest. He did not rebuke by looking at somebody's wealth, family, or power, but he would offer a person a remedy according to his own disease. For while the physicians of the body look at the diseases—and, accordingly, how often [42.10] do they cauterize the wealthy, operate on them, and make them fast, while they heal the poor with bread, delicate foods, and honey?—it would be very foolish for the physicians of souls to look at something other than the sicknesses themselves, and thus miss something that is necessary for the healing of him who is a common man or of him who is [42.15] held in honour.

49. Even if he advises in affairs of minor importance, then, the philosopher must not feel shame (when advising), for why should he, who is a philosopher, refuse to be outspoken? If he does not consider anything else besides virtue to be a good thing, what desire can beguile him and what fear can make him afraid? [42.20] More than anything, then, he should take care to use that strength, which he trusts and of which he is proud, against those who are armed and are celebrated among men, for he is guarded by that strength and will not seem in any respect to be deprived of it [43.1], weak, or held by praise, money, or desires.

50. To kings and princes, their rank provides the power to punish the wrong-doers, to the philosophers, the fact that they do not err gives them [43.5] the power to chastise the evil-doer. But if his soul is held in the passions, the trust in him abates and his fortitude grows cool, which should be a companion for him like a sword that is sharp and hangs from his heart.

51. When he intends to rebuke somebody, first he should look at his own person and say: 'Am [43.10] I also like one such?' Once he has examined himself and has found his soul to be removed from passions, only then shall he apply himself to healing others, lest that fable by Aesop shall be told to him: 'The animals told the frog who declared itself to be an expert in medicine: "How [43.15] can you attempt to heal others, when your own complexion is greenish?"' The philosopher's blemishes, however small, do not lie hidden, and he shall consider that, if he, though alone, sets his mind on the rest of men, the more the rest of men shall set their minds on him who is one; and this is even more so since [43.20] the philosopher does not have *a house or a household*, but produces everything by himself with his hands and is visible to all as though he were acting in a theatre. When one looks closely, on what statue can one not find a blemish?

52. As the philosopher has to be healthy in every respect, [43.25] he must also guard humility and severity within himself, [44.1] both of which are excellences of the soul, so that he may bestow humility on the humble and

severity on the evil. The people of the Athenians dubbed Diogenes 'dog' because his couch was on the ground and he [44.5] used to spend the night on the streets in front of the doors. Diogenes, however, liked this appellation for he saw that it resembled his deeds. You know what Plato relates about the nature of dogs. He relates that they wag their tail and love those whom they know, but they [44.10] rage at those whom they do not know; and they set apart enemies and friends not from the fact that they are good or bad towards them, but by whether they know or do not know somebody.[32] The philosopher, then, must not love the person who gives him a present or hate the person who does not donate him a gift [44.15], but he must regard as a friend the person in whom he sees virtue, and he shall perceive that a person is a stranger on account of the fact that he sees evil in him. Indeed, to the dog the faculty was given to recognize friends through customary sight, but to the philosopher was given the intellect in addition to his eyes [44.20] so that, having set apart friend from enemy, he may draw the latter near to himself and set the former further away, not to fulfil his anger or to bite, but to conquer him and heal him through admonition, and to remove the hidden blemishes through his admonition as through a bite and to lay them in the open. The person who [44.25] acts like a dog in this way does not merely guard a house or [45.1] the person who feeds him, but he is a guard to all

32. Plato *Republic Book* 2, 375E.

men, not lest they lose their possessions, but lest righteousness and concord are pillaged from them.

53. For this reason the Athenians honoured Crates greatly. The story relates that [45.5] Crates used to go from house to house where there was tumult and irritation, and he did not leave until he had produced concord among the people.[33]

1.6. COMPARATIVE FREEDOM OF SPEECH FOR PHILOSOPHERS IN PRE-ISLAMIC SIXTH-CENTURY PERSIAN AND ISLAMIC TENTH–THIRTEENTH CENTURY ARABIC

By the sixth century, the empire of the Christian emperor Justinian in Constantinople was securely Christian and he shut down teaching in the Athenian Neoplatonist school of philosophy in 529, because its ideas were at variance with Christianity. His emphasis on putting an end to teaching represented an animus against freedom of speech. By contrast, the pre-Islamic Persian king, Anūshirwān, Khushru I, in the first year of his reign, 531 CE, invited the Athenians to come and discuss with him ten questions he raised about Greek philosophy and science. King Khushru gave them refuge. The *Answers to King Khosroes* is now translated into English for the first time

---

33. Diogenes Laertius, *Lives of Eminent Philosophers*, 6.86; Apuleius, *Florida* 22; Julian, *Oration* 6, 201B–C.

by a team with expertise in Greek science and in reconstructing the lost original Greek from a Latin translation which misunderstood both the Greek and the Science.[34]

When the Athenians left, Khushru enforced a treaty with the Christian emperor who had stopped their teaching, a treaty in which he required that the emperor leave them unmolested when they returned to their homes. He was thus ensuring other freedoms as well as the freedom to continue doing philosophy. After the Athenians departed, he continued to invite other Greek philosophers (Agathias *Hist.* 2.29.9).[35] One, Ouranius, was a sceptic (2.29.7) of the kind that the Athenian Neoplatonists would themselves have considered no philosopher at all, because sceptics of this kind avoided believing in anything, even the existence of philosophy, and therefore had the reputation of mere controversialists. But Khushru had him debate with Zoroastrians on such subjects as the eternity or otherwise of the universe, the analysis of coming into existence, nature, and whether one should posit a single first principle (*arkhē*, 2.29.11).[36] He further had Nestorian Christians debate with Monophysite Christians and, upon losing the debate, to stop disparaging them (2.29.11). Khushru was also the earliest person of whom I know to have had a Sanskrit work

---

34. Priscian, *Answers to King Khosroes of Persia*, in the series Ancient Commentators on Aristotle, Bloomsbury Academic, London, 2016.

35. Agathias, *Histories*, 2.29. See especially Michel Tardieu, 'Chosroes', in R. Goulet, ed., *Dictionnaire des philosophes antiques*, vol. 2, CNRS Éditions, Paris 1994, pp. 309–318, at pp. 311, 312, 315, 317; Joel. T. Walker, 'The limits of late antiquity: Philosophy between Rome and Iran', *The Ancient World* 33, 2002, pp. 45–69.

36. Agathias, *Histories* 2.29.11.

translated into Persian: the Aesop-like moral tales about animals of the *Pancatantra*. His interest in diverse cultures thus took the form of posing questions, arranging debates, and seeking translations.

Finally, two Persian accounts of Aristotelian logic by Paul the Persian were dedicated to Khushru. Paul preserved the Greek tradition, culminating in Alexandria, of writing introductions to Philosophy and to Aristotelian logic, and he addressed two such writings to Khushru. I have argued elsewhere that he studied in Alexandria with the Greek philosopher Philoponus.[37] Paul's work had enduring influence, being available in Syriac in the sixth century[38] and in Arabic by the early tenth century, where it influenced Muslim and Christian philosophers alike. Dimitri Gutas has conjectured[39] that it was known in Arabic to the Muslims al-Fārābī in the tenth century and Miskawayh in the eleventh. Paul was a Nestorian Christian at the time he instructed Khushru in Philosophy, but it is said, whether reliably or not, that, on failing to become Metropolitan Bishop of Persia, he abandoned Christianity and that he converted to Zoroastrianism.[40]

---

37. Richard Sorabji, 'The cross-cultural spread of Greek philosophy (and Indian moral tales) to 6th century Persian and Syriac', *Studia Graeco-Arabica* 9, 2019, pp. 147–163.

38. The Syriac survives and there is also a Latin translation in Jan Pieter Nicolaas Land, ed., *Anecdota Syriaca*, vol. 4, Brill, Leiden, 1875, pp. 1–30.

39. Dimitri Gutas, 'Paul the Persian on the classification of the parts of Aristotle's philosophy: A milestone between Alexandria and Baghdad', *Der Islam* 60, 1983, pp. 231–267.

40. The source for the first claim is the *Chronicle of Seert* (a ninth–eleventh-century history in Arabic of Nestorian Christianity), for the second, a thirteenth-century

Khushru himself was a Zoroastrian, but had a Christian wife, and is on record as having said in his account of his deeds, *Kārnāmag*:

> We examined the customs of our forebears, but, con-
> cerned with the discovery of the truth, we [also] studied
> the customs and conduct of the Romans [i.e. Justinian's
> Constantinople empire] and Indians and accepted those
> among them which seemed reasonable and praiseworthy,
> not merely likeable. We have not rejected anyone because
> they belonged to a different religion or people. And hav-
> ing examined the good customs and laws of our ancestors
> as well as those of the foreigners, we have not declined to
> adopt anything which was good nor to avoid anything
> which was bad. Affection for our forebears did not lead us
> to accept customs which were not good.

Similar freedom was found when Greek philosophical ideas passed between the eighth and tenth centuries to Muslims and Christians in the Arabic-speaking world. In tenth century Baghdad, the Muslim philosopher al-Fārābī was free to side with Aristotle, against the apparent sense of the Koran, in say-ing that the universe had no beginning. Fārābī was a philoso-pher not only in our sense, but in the sense of subordinating

Syrian bishop, Barhebraeus. See in Goulet, *Dictionnaire des philosophes antiques*, the entries 'Chosroes' by M. Tardieu, vol. II, p. 315, and 'Paul le Perse' by H. Hugonnard-Roche, vol. Va, p. 184.

scriptural doctrines to intellectual thought, including that of Aristotle. By contrast, al-Ghazālī in the eleventh century, whom we would regard as a very good philosopher, counted as a theologian instead. His *Destruction of the Philosophers*, as it is sometimes translated, is directed not only against Fārābī in the tenth century, but also against Avicenna in the eleventh century as a philosopher, and his list of objections to the so-called philosophers gives us an idea of what the philosophers were free to teach. They could follow Aristotle in denying a beginning of the universe (as did Fārābī), individual survival after death, and God's knowledge of particulars. So long as they did not deny the existence of prophets or their role in society, they could deny these things without being persecuted. Despite al-Ghazālī's forceful objections, he was succeeded by other philosophers, and one of them, Averroes in the twelfth century, could write with impunity against Ghazālī in *The Destruction of the Destruction*.[41] Faisal Devji tells me that Modern Islam has a similar approach in allowing different views about the characteristics of God, but objecting to any diminution of the Prophet or recognition of other comparable prophets.[42]

Averroes also wrote on law and, as Noah Feldman has pointed out,[43] he used Aristotle to deal with a disputed

---

41. Further details again in the introduction to Richard Sorabji, ed., *Aristotle Reinterpreted*, Bloomsbury, London, 2016.
42. Faisal Devji, 'Free speech controversies about Islam', Talk at St Antony's College, Oxford, 22 November 2016.
43. Noah Feldman, 'War and reason in Maimonides and Averroes', in Richard Sorabji and David Rodin, eds., *The Ethics of War: Shared Problems in Different Traditions*, Ashgate, Aldershot, 2006, Ch. 5, pp. 92–107.

question on whether Muslims should seek to kill all polytheists (this would not include Christians or Jews), or whether a truce should be allowed. Two verses of the Koran (9:5; 9:29) were believed to support killing, one (8:61) to allow truce, and it had been asked which verses superseded which. Averroes points out that it is impossible for Muslims to uproot their enemies entirely and it would do harm to try. He cites Aristotle *Nicomachean Ethics* 5.7, 1137b22–23, which insists that judges must be allowed discretion to correct the generalizations of laws in order to fit particular circumstances. The war verses, he suggests, express a general policy; the peace verse requires judicial discretion to meet particular circumstances.

1.7. AKBAR AND THE MUGHAL DYNASTY IN INDIA: THE BENEFITS OF INTER-RELIGIOUS READING

In India, the Mughal emperor Akbar (1542–1605, emperor from 1556) had the two greatest religious epics of the Hindus adapted into Persian versions for his Muslim subjects to read, as recently analysed by Audrey Truschke.[44] First to be adapted was the *Mahabharata*, the account of the great war, which includes, among many other ethical discussions, the

---

44. Audrey Truschke, *Culture of Encounters: Sanskrit at the Mughal Court*, Columbia University Press, New York, and Penguin India, New Delhi, 2016. I shall use her translations, supplemented by those in Carl W. Ernst, 'Muslim studies of Hinduism? A reconsideration of Arabic and Persian translations from Indian languages', *Iranian Studies* 36, 2003, pp. 173–195, at 180–182.

Bhagavadgita, with its insistence on the warrior's duty to kill even his relatives, since duty must be undertaken without concern for the fruits of action. But the *Bhagavadgita* was severely truncated in the Persian version for Muslim readers, while in another part of the *Mahabharata* the advice to Yudishthira from his fatally wounded great-uncle Bhimsa, about how to rule, was expanded with quotations from Persian literature.

Akbar had the preface to the adaptation written in Persian by his vizier Abū al-Fazl, who enumerates Akbar's reasons for commissioning the adaptation. Some reasons are of particular interest. Throughout history, humans have been unenlightened (*Preface*, 3). But if good fortune showed hidden secrets to the soul of some poor Muslim, he was likely to be killed for revealing them. The religious elite who merely imitate tradition have been allowed in the past simply to use Islamic law against new insights. Akbar wanted (*Preface* 18) Muslims to stop quarrelling about doctrine with Muslims, and Hindus and Muslims to stop such quarrels with each other, and instead to become seekers after God or the Truth, and to try to correct themselves after becoming aware of each other's virtues and faults. The religious elite (*Preface* 19) think themselves authorities and have concealed the sayings of the wise. Akbar thought this could be cured by translation that used expressions clear enough for the masses, but were also pleasing to the elite, starting with the Hindu *Mahabharata*. That great work, with its belief in an eternal past, could show Muslims the antiquity of the world and make them give up their belief in recent creation.

But similarly the Hindu religious elite have excessive faith in their religion, and they too take the path of blind imitation. Once again, translation using clear expressions would restrain Muslim objectors, but also embarrass Hindu adherents about some of their beliefs and turn them into seekers after the Truth, or God. Admittedly (*Preface* 20), there are conflicting accounts of Creation in the *Mahabharata*, but the wise do not judge simply on the basis of those that are false. Rather, the wise will reject some, not understand other things, and accept yet others, but only after much study and the use of penetrating insight.

This is a remarkable statement made on Akbar's behalf and with his approval. It is not offering free speech, but it is enormously expanding the range of views that each religion should study, and it is calling for a different level of critical reflection, not dismissing a rival faith, because some of its ideas are false, but studying hard to find which of one's own are false, and which of the rival views are true. Indeed, one is to use what is right about the rival ideas, in order to correct one's own.

Akbar also had Christian Jesuits at his court, and they hoped to convert him, so cannot have understood that conversion was not his objective. He was very sympathetic to much of their viewpoint, but said he could not understand the Christian idea of the incarnation—God being made flesh in the person of Christ—nor that of the Trinity—there being one God with three persons. The Jesuits also misunderstood Akbar by saying that he was certainly not a Mahometan, but also not a native (Hindu), because he believed in the one Creator-God, despite worshipping the sun, and that many thought he aimed at making a new religion.[45] In fact, the Persian translation of the *Mahabharata* recognizes the plurality of gods, often incarnate gods, but the translation also speaks of the monotheistic God of Islam at a point where the original refers to the Hindu creator-god, Brahma.[46] I wonder if this was made easier by something with which Muslims could sympathize: the Hindu belief in one highest universal principle, not Brahma but Brahman, stressed in Hindu philosophy, a subject which Abū al-Faisal also summarized for Akbar. There seems to be a clash between the Jesuits' belief that there needs to be one religion which has got everything right, and Akbar's belief that each religion has some things wrong and some right, but that individuals can be helped by exposure to other religions to shed wrong beliefs and to come to accept some of what others have got right. That was Abū al-Fazl's account of the aim of Akbar's translation project.

The benefits Akbar is said to have sought from making other views available in translation are close to those which John Stuart Mill was later to expect from freedom of discussion in Chapter 2 of his classic *On Liberty*, to be considered in the following. It is not that Akbar allowed total freedom of speech. He required the Jains, who had broken away from

---

45. Reported from Father Xavier in *An Account of the Jesuit Missions to the Court of Akbar by Father Pierre Jarriq, S.J.*, translated by C. H Payne, Harper, New York and London, 1926, 28, cf. 67.

46. Truschke, *Sanskrit at the Mughal Court*, p. 115.

large parts of Hindu belief, to prove that they were not atheists. But he was open-minded enough to be persuaded that
they were not.[47] His most prolific translator, Badā'ūnī, who
in the mid-1580s translated some of the *Mahabharata*, and in
the later 1580s the whole of the other great religious epic, the
Ramayana, felt a tremendous weight suppressing his freedom
of speech. Akbar called him at one stage a bigot for following Islamic law, instead of open-minded versions of Sufism,
when he appeared to introduce into his translation the Muslim
belief in God's Day of Judgement. But at least Akbar was himself open enough to accept Badā'ūnī's explanation that the
original Sanskrit itself refers to periods spent in heaven or
hell. Badā'ūnī himself, however, belonged to the elite circle
of orthodox Sunni Muslim religious leaders, and in his own
very critical history of the period of Akbar, he describes the
Ramayana as heresy, which he disliked translating, but he was
commanded. However, he refused the royal command to add a
preface to it, parallel to Abū al-Fazl's preface to the translation
of the *Mahabharata*, because praise in the preface of the one
God, Allah, would have been forbidden—another limitation
on freedom of speech.[48]

Abū al-Fazl wrote another work for Akbar, the *Akbarnamah*,
whose third volume is called *Akbar's Institutes*, in five books.
The second section of Book 4, entitled *Learning of India*, expli-
cates six Hindu schools of philosophy, and distinguishes three

47. Truschke, *Sanskrit at the Mughal Court*, pp. 176–180.
48. Ibid., pp. 115, 206–207.

break-away groups, Jains, Buddhists, and atheists. The atheists are disparaged and the account of them truncated. But the Jains have the fullest treatment of all nine schools, and there were many Jains at Akbar's court. The Jains had dispensed with the Hindu focus on ritual, and had a view that allowed for a single, non-creator God, but also for the occasional incarnation of divine teachers. Their further view that everyone, apart from the divine teachers, has only partial knowledge of the truth (*Anekāntavāda*) would surely have fitted very well with Akbar's concern with the scouring for insights of views rival to one's own.

Akbar's grandson and potential heir to the throne Dārā Shukuh longed for the experience of union with a unitary God, and looked for this experience not only within Islam, but in other religions too. In the 1640s and 1650s, he commissioned the translation from Sanskrit into Persian of fifty Upanishads from Hindu scripture, regarding them as an explication of the Islamic monotheism of the Koran. He also attempted to translate into Persian the Hindus' *Bhagavadgita*. He further wrote a book with the title *The Meeting Place of the Two Oceans*, a phrase from the Koran, intending it as a meeting place for his preferred Islamic and Hindu mystical traditions. He also looked at the Jewish Torah, the psalms of David, and the Christian Gospels.[49] Unlike Akbar, he was making a particular selection

---

49. Yoginder Sikand, online publication, 'Beyond Hindu and Muslim: Dara Shikoh's quest for unity'; I am grateful to Shail Mayaram for the references to Sikand and, in the following, Kinra.

to suit his own personal interests, not to expand the insights of the common people. He regarded the selected Islamic and Hindu strands as expressing the same knowledge, rather than as calling for critical contrast and comparison. In his own words, 'I have written this investigation in accordance with my own mystical unveiling and experience for the sake of my own family, and I have nothing to do with the common people of either community'.[50] This does not sound like the words of an aspiring emperor, and it makes him unlike Akbar, who had a further project in having Hindu texts translated with the hope that his Muslim subjects would correct some of their mistakes. Dārā did, like Akbar, criticize the orthodox élite, the *ulema*, but for opposing his personal researches.

The disclaimer of intention to reform the common man, an interest found earlier in Akbar's documents, might sound like a precaution against orthodox critics, including his younger brother Aurungzeb, who had Dārā executed in 1659 on the pretext of un-Islamic activities and seized the throne. But Rajeev Kinra has argued for a different view,[51] that the Moghul dynasty, Aurungzeb included, had always talked with mystics of different religions and Aurungzeb was to be no exception. This is not to say that Aurungzeb was tolerant when it did not

---

50. Ernst, 'Muslim Studies of Hinduism', pp. 183–187; Truschke, *Sanskrit at the Mughal Court*, pp. 223–225.
51. R. Kinra, 'Infantilizing Bābā Dārā: The cultural memory of Dārā Shekuh and the Mughal public sphere', *Journal of Persianate Studies* 2, 2009, pp. 165–193. Yoginder Sikand, online publication, 'Beyond Hindu and Muslim: Dara Shikoh's quest for unity', http://www.svabhinava.org/meccabenares/YoginderSikand/DaraShikoh-frame.php

suit him, and he found excuses to have all three of his brothers executed. This was a convenient excuse for eliminating Dārā. Kinra's quotations from Dārā show him particularly captivated by mystical aspirations, and Kinra cites a report that in 1653 Dārā consulted the Hindu mystic Bābā Lāl, and argues that he consulted on how to combine mysticism with his princely calling. Kinra finds evidence that the mystical aspirations dominated over preparations for rule.

Jonardon Ganeri[52] has brought out that almost immediately after Dārā's death, a scholar formerly employed by Dārā, possibly Kavindra Sarasvati, was studying in a circle with François Bernier the philosophy from France of Descartes and of the atomist Gassendi, which Bernier had translated into Persian between 1658/9 and 1661/2. This intellectual study evidently did not attract the censorship of Aurungzeb.

1.8. A CONTRAST WITH HERESY IN CHRISTIANITY FROM THE THIRD CENTURY CE ONWARDS

I have traced elsewhere[53] the attitudes of Christians deemed mainstream towards Christians deemed heretics, starting from Tertullian (c. 160–220 CE). On the whole, heretics were

---

52. Jonardon Ganeri, *The Lost Age of Reason, Philosophy in Early Modern India 1450–1700*, Oxford University Press, Oxford, 2011, esp. pp. 13–59, 74–88.
53. Richard Sorabji, *Moral Conscience through the Ages*, Oxford University Press, Oxford, and the University of Chicago Press, Chicago, 2014, especially Ch. 3.

attacked for their beliefs, not merely for their outward speech, but speech was important in charges of blasphemy, in the banning of books and of certain statements, and in suppressing translations of the Bible.

1.9. THIRTEENTH–FOURTEENTH-CENTURY CONDEMNATIONS OF IDEAS AND BOOKS IN THE EUROPEAN UNIVERSITIES, INCLUDING BISHOP TEMPIER'S AT THE UNIVERSITY OF PARIS IN 1277

Bishop Tempier in 1277 condemned 219 propositions that were being disseminated in the Faculty of Arts in the University of Paris, along with a small number of books. One might not, for example, limit God's power by saying that he could not move the entire physical universe sideways, create as many worlds as he liked, or put different bodies in the very same place.[54] Some of the propositions condemned belonged to the Aristotelian tradition, and 1277 was only four years after the death of Thomas Aquinas, who had restored Aristotle and some of his commentators to providing a basis for understanding much Christian

---

54. See Edward Grant, 'The condemnation of 1277: God's absolute power and physical thought in the later Middle Ages', *Viator* 10, 1979, pp. 211–244, repr. in his *Studies in Medieval Science and Natural Philosophy*, London, 1981.

doctrine. In a careful survey article, covering recent discussion and drawing on his own book, Hans Thijssen has estimated that there were approximately sixteen condemnations of particular ideas at the University of Paris in the thirteenth to fourteenth centuries.[55] Other condemnations of errors in the thirteenth century included those in the same year of 1277, by Archbishop Robert Kilwardby at Oxford University.

1.10. ELEVENTH–FIFTEENTH-CENTURY RESTRICTION OF VERNACULAR TRANSLATIONS OF THE BIBLE, COUNTERED BY PROTESTANT SIXTEENTH-CENTURY TRANSLATIONS, IN TURN ANSWERED BY THE CATHOLIC INDEX OF BANNED BOOKS FROM THE COUNCIL OF TRENT

Translations of the Bible, especially of the Old Testament, into contemporary languages were not numerous after the tenth century, and all translations were restricted to authorized versions from 1199 by Pope Innocent III, to

---

55. J. M. M. H. Thijssen, 'Condemnation of 1277', *Stanford Encyclopaedia of Philosophy*, http://plato.stanford.edu/entries/condemnation/ (with bibliography), and *Censure and Heresy at the University of Paris, 1200–1400*, University of Pennsylvania Press, Philadelphia, 1998.

guard against the spread of heresies. This meant that those without Latin or other necessary languages depended on accepted authorities for interpretations. The restriction on vernacular translations curtailed the free speech only of the few potential translators, but reduced discussion for whole populations. As regards English translations, John Wyclif in Oxford in 1383 produced a handwritten translation of the whole Bible in a good many copies. But he avoided execution possibly only through his dying soon after in 1384, and his translation was banned in 1408. Jan Hus, who supported his work, was burnt at the stake in 1415. John Colet's translation was displayed in St Paul's Cathedral in 1496, and was seen by thousands. But when Tyndale produced a printed translation in much larger numbers in 1526, by moving from England to Germany and later to Antwerp and shifting from one printing press to another, he was strangled and burned in 1536. In the sixteenth century, however, Protestants made translations into many languages, and in England a corner was turned three years after Tyndale's death, when, under King Henry VIII, every church was required to make available the Great Bible commissioned by Thomas Cranmer. Even after that, Cranmer was burnt at the stake in Oxford in 1556, under the Catholic Queen Mary Tudor.

After the Protestant Reformation, the Roman Catholic Church established at the Council of Trent in 1560 a general index of books not to be read by the faithful, to protect them from heresy or immorality. It was abolished it in 1966.

1.11. THE NEW SEVENTEENTH-CENTURY DEMANDS IN ENGLAND OF JOHN MILTON

I come now to the earliest European pleas I know for free speech for everyone. They came later than pleas for freedom of conscience or religion, which I have discussed elsewhere.[56] Although restriction on these earlier freedoms had had implications for speech, that was not yet the main focus of complaint. Even when implemented, freedom of speech tends to spread to some groups more slowly than others, to women, for example, more slowly than to men. It is still a question how far women have in practice attained in the United Kingdom equal freedom of speech in all contexts, and in India I was recently reminded by a Dalit that his community had not attained it. The example has been given of Dalits not being heard in village councils.[57]

The seventeenth century, rather than the sixteenth,[58] may mark a new beginning in Europe. The first European demand I know of for widespread free speech, in particular for unlicensed publication, was made earlier in England by John Milton in 1644, in his *Areopagitica*, a speech for the liberty of

---

56. Sorabji, *Moral Conscience through the Ages*.
57. Arvind Kejriwal, *Swaraj*, Harper Collins, India, 2012, pp. 95–97.
58. My attention has been drawn to Montaigne's sixteenth-century *Essay* III. 8, *On the Art of Conversation* (*conferer*). But although Montaigne mentions truth, his scepticism about finding it shows through. He described his delight at conversation with someone who can refute him, but he still says that this is only a quest, the fun is in the chase and only God's knowledge possesses truth.

unlicensed printing. King Charles I from his accession in 1625 had rigorously enforced the old requirement of prior license for any publication through use of the dreaded Court of the Star Chamber, until 1640, when he had to bargain with Parliament for funds for pursuing the civil war, and Parliament abolished the Court and briefly printing flourished. But already William Prynne had been imprisoned for printing tracts against bishops in the late 1620s, as was John Bastwick in 1633–1634, and the printer Henry Overton had been brought before the Ecclesiastical Commission in 1632 and 1633 for printing religious tracts.[59] This was before the imprisonment of the future Levellers, to whom we shall come, starting with that of John Lilburne in 1639. These legal proceedings were all concerned with religion, and that was also the centre of Milton's interest[60] when he responded to Parliament, dominated by Presbyterian protestants, reintroducing prior licensing in 1643. Milton's arguments in response to the renewed censorship of printing included the point that at first Church councils and bishops had merely declared what books were not commendable, leaving it to people's conscience whether they would read them. Prior licensing was first required by the Roman Church. But knowledge of *vice* and rejection of its supposed benefits are necessary for virtue, and the scanning of *error* is necessary to the confirmation of truth. Moreover, licensers are hacks inferior to

---

59. John Rees, *The Leveller Revolution*, Verso, London, 2016, pp. 28–29.
60. I am grateful to Faramerz Dabhoiwala for stressing this point to me, as well as urging me to discuss Milton's well-known exclusion of Catholics from his freedoms.

the writers they censor. If only received opinion is allowed, we lose great men like Galileo.

Important though this was, there were, however, certain weaknesses in Milton's case. He argued, for example, that truth would always prevail in a contest with falsehood. This was optimistic even then, and in chapter 3 it will be considered further in connection with today's media landscape, particularly social media. But Milton's other arguments in *Areopagitica* did not depend on his over-optimism, and he also went on to repeat his call for discussion and listening to the other side, without letting it rest on his over-optimistic assurance.

Another very startling feature of Milton's discussion, however, is that he openly excluded Catholics from his provisions for freedom. But I think that he had a real problem to face, which has recurred in other contexts, and which few knew how to answer. What freedoms do you allow to those whose record shows they would stop freedoms, including freedom of speech, if they were in office? Certainly Anglicans and Presbyterians had been stopping freedoms too. But Catholic rulers were seen as subservient to a foreign power, the Pope, and the reign of the last Catholic sovereign, Mary, was remembered as particularly bloody. Nowadays, too, some people are asking whether a democracy, by letting in a populist leader who flouts democratic conventions, can lead to tyranny, as Plato had said it would in Book IX of his *Republic* and as Aristotle confirmed with historical examples and general explanations, adding that the worst of his four kinds of democracy was already a tyranny, in which the law was overridden by decrees.[61] His preferred constitution was a mixture of democratic rule by the poor with rule by the rich, inclining towards the democratic side,[62] but with each side kept from aggrandizement by a large middle class.[63]

Very special circumstances were needed for Milton to be able to make his demand for freedom to publish. England was engaged from 1641 to 1646 in the first of two civil wars against King Charles I and his royalist supporters. Both civil wars were to be lost by the King's side, the second in 1648. Milton had earlier objected to the authority of bishops in the Anglican Church and switched for a time to the Presbyterians, whose priests were elected to a church by the church's congregation. But in 1646, when the Presbyterians in Parliament abolished the institution of Anglican bishops, he finished his poem 'On the new forces of conscience under the Long Parliament' by saying: 'New Presbyter is but old priest writ large', and thereafter he urged the independence of Church from State.

In the second civil war of 1648, the king was offered an alliance by the Presbyterian Parliament, with the aim of establishing Presbyterianism. But when this was defeated by the victorious Model Army, in temporary alliance with the Levellers, the victors had Parliament stripped of the king's Presbyterian supporters in what was known as Pride's Purge,

61. Aristotle, *Politics*, Book 4, ch. 4; cf. Book 4, ch. 3; Book 5, ch. 5; Book 6, chs 4–5.
62. Aristotle, *Politics*, Book 4, ch. 5, 1293b, 33–38.
63. Aristotle *Politics*, Book 4, ch. 11.

after Thomas Pride who conducted the arrests at the door of Parliament. In January 1649, the Model Army beheaded the king himself and declared a Commonwealth in place of the monarchy. The remaining 'Rump' Parliament ruled under the influence of the Model Army's most senior officers, the 'Independents', Fairfax and Oliver Cromwell. In 1649, Milton, with his numerous languages, took over the role of foreign secretary to the Commonwealth. Even so, the success of Milton's side was reversed, when in 1660 the monarchy was restored. Milton went into hiding for sixteen weeks, but suffered less than others, with brief imprisonment and a fine and an order by Parliament for two of his books to be burnt. Dying in 1674, he did not live to see the restored dynasty replaced in 1688 by William III of Orange, who was invited over as king from that haven of comparatively free speech, Holland. Milton would not, however, have been likely to approve the continuation of rule by one man, or the Bill of Rights of 1689 introduced under William, which required freedom of speech only for debates in Parliament.

From 1653 to his death in 1658, Oliver Cromwell, a commander in the victorious army and already the most prominent figure in the Commonwealth, but now fresh from further conquests in Ireland and Scotland, accepted the role of Lord Protector and the Commonwealth became a Protectorate. The next year, 1654, Milton wrote his *Second Defence of the English People* with a defence of Oliver Cromwell, but also an admonition 'to permit the free discussion of truth without any hazard to the author, or any subjection to the caprice of an individual', adding 'which is the best way to make truth flourish and knowledge abound'. This develops the point that the scanning of error is necessary to the confirmation of truth, which he had made in his *Areopagitica*.

After the restoration of the monarchy in 1660, Milton wrote his most famous epic poems and returned to political writing only in 1673, the year before his death, with his *Of True Religion*. There he argued that one of the safeguards against Popery, that is, Roman Catholicism, was to tolerate other opinions, hear them patiently, and examine them. Moreover, he repeated for a third time his argument about the best route to truth: reading controversies sharpens judgement and confirms truth already recognized.

1.12. THE SEVENTEENTH-CENTURY LEVELLERS

Freedom of speech was not merely advocated during and after the English civil wars of 1641–1646 and 1648; it was practised. It has been said that during this period it became clear that many ordinary people had all along not believed what was said by priests or judges, but were only now free to say so.[64]

---

64. Of the many books on the period, a path-breaking one was Christopher Hill, *The World Turned Upside Down: Radical Ideas during the English Revolution*, Maurice Temple-Smith, London, 1982, Penguin, Harmondsworth, UK, 1985. I am

Perhaps the most striking case was that of the Levellers, many of them long since active in the late 1630s to 1640s before the name 'Leveller' was coined in 1647.[65] Some of them had been members of the New Model Army, which was to defeat the king's supporters, and later in 1648–1649 the Levellers were to become briefly allies of that army. Before that, in 1647, they engaged in the first of two debates with Oliver Cromwell and his son-in-law, Henry Ireton, both senior officers of the Model Army, to which some Levellers belonged. Both debates lasted several days and both were very fully recorded.[66] The first debate was held in Putney from 28 October to 1 November 1647 and concerned the Levellers' call for democratic reforms. Some of the reforms called for then or later were not to be implemented for three hundred years, or not even then: giving the vote to all freeborn and constraining the power of parliaments by reducing their tenure to two years.

The second debate with the Levellers concerned freedom of conscience in religious belief and practice, and was held in Whitehall on 14 December 1648 and 8–11 and 13 January 1649, very shortly after Pride's Purge of Parliament, which removed the Presbyterian supporters of the king. Also in December 1648, John Lilburne, perhaps the best known of the Levellers, proposed to Cromwell that *An Agreement of the*

drawing on a sketch of the seventeenth century in my *Moral Conscience through the Ages*, Ch. 8.

65. John Rees, *The Leveller Revolution*, pp. 138, 154.
66. A. S. P. Woodhouse, *Puritanism and Liberty, Being the Army Debates (1647–9) from the Clarke Manuscripts*, Dent and Sons, London, 1938, 3rd edition, 1986.

People should be drawn up. His own published version, with a print run claimed to be of 20,000, announced the dissolution of the current Parliament by April 1649, and its replacement by 'representatives of the people'. Its clause number 7 concerned freedom of conscience. Learning that Ireton and the army had already submitted to Parliament their own recommendations from the first debate, he published his second draft on 16 December 1648, as 'Second Agreement of the People'. He claimed that his draft conformed to what had been agreed in the Putney debate, except—on one point—by Ireton. Clause 7 on freedom of conscience now included a part on conscientious objection to military conscription. Firstly, the people's representatives (who were to succeed the present Parliament) must allow worship in accordance with conscience, though at their discretion they could offer the nation public direction in religion, provided it was non-compulsive and did not support what was regarded as intolerant: Roman Catholicism ('Popery'), or the Church of England system of priests headed by bishops ('Anglicanism'). Secondly, they could not press-gang people into war, if war, or even that *particular* war, was against their conscience. Thirdly, there should be an amnesty for all except those whom the present Parliament chose to punish for supporting the king.

Although the Levellers were calling for freedom of conscience and religion, their doing so face to face with Cromwell and in books and pamphlets against strong opposition meant that they were also exercising freedom of *speech*. The new name 'Leveller' was introduced by their opponents to signify that they were making everyone level. But on one estimate, they were already an identifiable group by 1645, with a printed manifesto of July 1646, *A Remonstrance of Many Thousand Citizens and Other Freeborn People of England.*[67] Many of them had been active as individuals well before Milton wrote in support of free publication in 1644. Already in 1639 John Lilburne had published *A Cry for Justice*, and in 1641 *The Christian Mans Triall*, and a woman Leveller, Katherine Chidley, *The Justification of the Independent Churches.*[68] Women, including wives of the leading men, continued to play a major role, in a further sign of equality.[69] In 1646 Elizabeth Lilburne forced her way into Westminster to present a petition to the House of Commons for her husband's release from one of his imprisonments, and in 1647 Mary Overton was caught binding her Leveller husband's books in her home. In 1649 there was a series of petitions, some reprinted in *The Moderate*, for the release of leading men of the Levellers. The *Humble petition of divers wel-affected Women*, supposedly with 10,000 signatures, was brought to Westminster by 500 women, twenty of whom broke into the lobby of the House of Commons.

The Levellers had lost the only senior officer of the Model Army to support them fully when Thomas Rainsborough was murdered by a raiding party of Royalists in 1648.[70]

67. Rees, *The Leveller Revolution*, pp. 128–129, 138, 141, 151, 154.
68. Ibid., pp. 32, 38.
69. For the role of women, see Rees, *The Leveller Revolution*, index, *s.v.* 'Women'.
70. Rees, *The Leveller Revolution*, pp. 155, 261–265.

Disillusioned by the back-tracking of which they complained in their former allies, the leaders of the New Model Army, the Levellers in 1649 eventually resorted to mutinies in a series of towns. Cromwell defeated them in Burford in Oxfordshire, with negotiations in that town uncompleted. He imprisoned the survivors in Burford Church, where the name of one prisoner is still inscribed in the lead of the font, and had three of them shot outside. The movement had lasted four or five years.

1.13. HOLLAND AS A SAFE PLACE FOR PUBLISHING AND FOR RETREAT

Tolerance for freedom of expression in the form of public worship was better exemplified in Holland than in England for much of the seventeenth century. As Holland gradually drove back south the Spanish invaders, who were Catholics, William I of Orange repeatedly called for religious freedom from as early as 1575, and in 1579 wrote into the Union of Utrecht that 'each person shall remain free, especially in his religion, and that no one shall be persecuted or investigated because of his religion'. In 1639, the imprisoned future Leveller John Lilburne sent his *Cry for Justice*, addressed to English sympathizers, for secret printing in *Holland*, to avoid the legal censorship of the Stationer's Company at home.[71]

71. Ibid., pp. 32, 68.

Towards the later end of the seventeenth century, Holland was a haven of freedom for political writers in general. John Locke retreated there from England from 1683 to 1688. Pierre Bayle escaped to Holland from Catholic persecution in France, and the home-born Spinoza from a Portuguese community in Holland, expelled as an atheist from his Jewish community, acknowledged the benefit of State tolerance. All exercised freedom of speech by writing in ways their home communities did not allow. All supported freedom of religion and conscience. It may seem that Spinoza addressed more directly than the others the topic of freedom of speech in Chapter 20 of his *Theological-Political Treatise* in 1670. He distinguished between judgements, speech, and acts. The sovereign powers of a state have the right to control only acts against the law. The stability of the State does not require control of judgements nor of speech, except for speech that would dissolve the agreement to surrender the right to *act* contrary to the laws. Any attempt to allow judgements, while forbidding their spoken expression, will have disastrous consequences for the State. But stability does require the law-abiding to submit to the sovereign any speech against the current laws. This may sound like a comparatively small restriction, but it begins to look much larger, when we take Ch. 20 together with Chapter 19.[72] For there the sovereign makes the laws not just about civil behaviour, but also about

---

72. I owe this observation to Maria Rosa Antognazza, 'Truth and Toleration in Early Modern Thought'. In Ian Hunter and Richard Whatmore (eds), *Philosophy, Rights and Natural Law*. Edinburgh: Edinburgh University Press, 2019, pp. 36–70.

religious practice; thus one needs the sovereign's permission to speak against his decisions on religious practice. This no longer looks so like a defence of free speech.

Leibniz (1646–1716), Spinoza's contemporary, has been presented as far more tolerant than Spinoza and he did not need to go into exile. His discussions are scattered in letters, and on the whole he was opposing persecution of opinion, but only one explicit expression of freedom of *speech* has been brought to my attention, the freedom to write (and that without any distinct rationale).[73] Moreover, the propagation of pernicious doctrine he is prepared to punish, albeit as mildly as possible, but even by exile, provided that there is another country to go to.[74]

Pierre Bayle, another exile in Holland, provided the only good answer I have seen to Milton's earlier problem in the seventeenth century. He did so in 1686, in Part 1 of his *Philosophical Commentary on These Words of Jesus Christ,*

---

73. Maria Rosa Antognazza, 'Truth and toleration in early modern thought', and 'Leibniz's doctrine of toleration, philosophical, theological and pragmatic reasons', in J. Parkin and T. Stanton, eds., *Natural Law and Toleration in the Early Enlightenment*, Proceedings of the British Academy, 186, Oxford University Press, Oxford, 2013, pp. 139–164. The second paper, p. 162, draws attention to Leibniz's remark of 21 July 1707, quoted there about the Jansenist Gerberon: 'And indeed, if it were within my powers of persuasion, Gerberon and others like him would enjoy complete freedom . . . let them write, let them defend their opinions. Their errors should be overturned with equal arms, not by force and fear'; taken from Leibniz, *Die philosophischen Schriften*, II, p. 337, trans. by Brandon C. Look and Donald Rutherford, in *The Leibniz–Des Bosses Correspondence*, Yale University Press, New Haven, CT, and London, 2007, pp. 95–97.

74. Antognazza, 'Leibniz's doctrine of toleration', p. 163, notes 98, 99, citing texts of 1706 and 1687.

'*Compel them to come in*'. A Hugenuot Protestant whose brother had died, imprisoned at the time of the 'Convertists' in the reign of the Catholic king of France Louis XIV, he escaped to Holland. But unlike Milton, Bayle showed genuine concern for the personal welfare of Catholics, should they be a minority in a country, as they would by then have been in Holland. They must be allowed to believe and practise their religion, and teach it to their children. One should not enforce or reward their changing religion, nor abuse their persons, impair or confiscate their property, or restrict their access to the law. But equally they should not be allowed to force the consciences of others. Moreover, laws are needed to stop them meddling and disturbing the state.

1.14. FROM MADISON'S FIRST AMENDMENT OF 1791 TO THE FOURTEENTH AMENDMENT OF 1868 IN THE UNITED STATES

I move now to eighteenth- and nineteenth-century America. I am throughout indebted to the explanations offered me by the late Daniel Robinson in the Philosophy Faculty of Oxford University,[75] who saw my final draft. The First Amendment did not require freedom of speech for individuals, let alone all

---

75. Including on Madison's draft Amendments, his *Remonstrance* and the contrast with the Fourteenth Amendment.

individuals. That came only with the Fourteenth Amendment of 1868.

I believe that the United States' First Amendment, as reinterpreted by the Supreme Court since the early twentieth century, is a noble idea, giving to all American citizens through freedom of speech a role in national politics, which is lacking in the United Kingdom,[76] where now citizens may feel they have a role only once in five years at parliamentary elections, or more of a role if the government uncharacteristically offers a binding referendum. But free speech had received no mention in the original US Constitution, which came into force in March 1789. Madison's first draft on 8 June 1789, of the Amendments to the Constitution, which collectively became the Bill of Rights, attempted to secure freedom of speech for individuals: 'The people shall not be deprived or abridged of their right to speak or to write, or to publish their sentiments'. But the final version of the First Amendment of 1791 did not require freedom of speech for individuals, but merely debarred Congress from dictating to the *States* decisions on freedom of speech. Part of the explanation can be found in the Introduction to Madison's first and rejected draft in June 1789 of proposed amendments[77] to the Constitution, which had been operating since March 1789. The first draft of Madison's Amendments emphasized that two

---

76. It has been put to me that a sign of its also dwindling in the US presidential elections of 2012 and 2016 is the strong preference expressed for candidates offering change.

77. Currently available at http://www.let.rug.nl/usa/presidents/james-madison/proposed-amendments-to-the-constitution.php

individual States, fearing an overbearing federal authority, had declined to join the federation, and by confining restrictions largely to the Congress he hoped to meet this anxiety. It will have been necessary for Madison to rebalance the position he had taken in the first of his Federalist papers of 1787–1788, the 10th, following others by Hamilton and Jay, and designed to persuade the people of New York State to support a Union of States. He had then argued that a republic electing representatives from a much larger territory would be better for *minorities* than the direct popular vote of the individual State in which a local majority faction could outvote a local minority. This had treated the individual State as a potential threat to its individual members. But now the First Amendment needed to reassure the States by leaving to them decisions on both freedom of religion and freedom of speech.

Madison's first draft of proposed amendments still sought to protect individuals as well as States, requiring of the Federal Government that:

Fourthly, . . . The people shall not be deprived or abridged of their right to speak, to write, or to publish their sentiments; and the freedom of the press, as one of the great bulwarks of liberty, shall be inviolable.

The people shall not be restrained from peaceably assembling and consulting for their common good, nor from applying to the legislature by petitions, or remonstrances for redress of their grievances.

Fifthly, . . . no state shall violate the equal rights of conscience, or the freedom of the press, or the trial by jury in
criminal cases.

In a later draft amendment, Madison distinguished freedom
of the press from the other freedoms of speech, explaining that
press freedom was more likely to be infringed by the States than
by the confederacy, which was less powerful. Despite Madison's
extra constraints on the States to ensure press freedom, the
version which eventually passed, after a series of debates, as
the First Amendment in 1791 required non-interference only
from Congress, while granting freedom not explicitly to individuals, but to individual *States*, allowing them to decide what
speech was allowable and what not. The First Amendment also
connected freedom of speech with freedom of religion, assembly, and petition, being formulated as follows: 'Congress shall
make no law respecting an establishment of religion, or pro-
hibiting the free exercise thereof; or abridging the freedom of
speech, or of the press; or the right of the people peaceably to
assemble, and to petition the government for a redress of grievances'. Madison had already shown particular anxiety about
religious freedom in 1785, two years before he started drafting
his Amendments. In his eloquent *Remonstrance* against a bill
for the General Assembly to privilege with payment teachers
of the Christian Religion, he included the plea: 'Who does not
see that the same authority which can establish Christianity,

in exclusion of all other Religions, may establish with the same ease any particular sect of Christians, in exclusion of all other sects?' His concern with freedom for rival religious persuasions may have drawn his attention to some of the connections between freedom of religion and freedom of speech.

Freedom of speech and of the press did not mean that publication could not be subsequently punished if it broke other laws. But there was no need to obtain a license for publication in advance. Thomas Jefferson in America in his second inaugural address in 1805, and Thomas Paine in *Commentaries on the Laws of England*[78] in 1806, like William Blackstone before them in England in 1765, though all rejecting censorship or *prior* restraint of the press or publications, nonetheless all insisted that the authors would be answerable *afterwards* for what they published, if it was criminal (Blackstone), or violated laws provided by the *States* against false and defamatory publications (Jefferson). Even Paine in 'Of the term "Liberty of the Press"' required answerability for saying atrocious things whether in one's own person or through the press.[79]

It was not until the Fourteenth Amendment in 1868 that the restrictions of the first eight Amendments on the rights

---

78. William Blackstone, *Facsimile of First Edition of 1765–9*, vol. 4, Chicago University Press, Chicago, 1979, p. 151.
79. So Onora O'Neill, *Speech Rights and Speech Wrongs*, Van Gorcum, Amsterdam, 2016, p. 18,

of Congress to make laws were 'incorporated', or imposed on the individual States. The motivating force as regards the Fourteenth Amendment proposed in 1866 was a new one: strengthening the rights that the Federal Government's Thirteenth Amendment in 1865 had provided in outlawing slavery at the end of the American Civil War. The States were now impeded in silencing the campaign for the abolition of slavery, and no State could have laxer laws than others as regards the rights of slaves. In February and April 1866, the Joint Committee on (post–Civil-War) Reconstruction voted in support of drafts of John Bingham's Fourteenth Amendment, which focused on the rights of individual citizens, not of individual States. The first draft read, 'The Congress shall have the power to make all laws which shall be necessary and proper to secure to the citizens of each state all privileges and immunities of citizens in the several states', and later in April in the closing debate in Congress, Bingham explained that cruel and unusual punishments had been inflicted under State laws in certain States.[80] The Fourteenth Amendment was unlike the First in protecting the freedom of speech of individuals and of all individuals, including former slaves.

---

80. On the effect of the Fourth Amendment, see Michael Sandel, *Democracy's Discontent*, Harvard University Press, Cambridge, MA, 1996, pp. 36–39. Differences between the effects of the First Amendment and of the Fourteenth in its new abolitionist context are discussed by Akhil Reed Amar, 'The creation and reconstruction of the First Amendment', Ch. 3 in Daniel N. Robinson and Richard N. Williams, eds., *Religious Liberty: Essays on First Amendment Law*, Cambridge University Press, Cambridge, 2016, pp. 36–63.

1.15. FREE SPEECH AS A RIGHT, THOUGH SUBJECT TO PENALTY: THOMAS PAINE, 1791–1792, AND HIS DEFENDER, LORD ERSKINE

Thomas Paine, in absence from England, published *The Rights of Man* in two parts in 1791 and 1792, praising the creation of a constitution in the French and American revolutions and criticizing the hereditary monarchy of England. His main interest was not freedom of speech, but he did cite the French Declaration of the Rights of Man and Citizen of 1789, which treated free speech as a *right*, subject to retrospective penalty. It did so in the following Article 11: 'The free communication of ideas and opinions is one of Man's most precious rights: every citizen is therefore free to speak, write and publish freely, except to answer for abuses to this liberty, in cases determined by the law'. The last was another boundary and a retrospective one. Paine argued against his English opponent Burke's claim that he should be subject to criminal prosecution. He replied, 'It would be an act of despotism, or what in England is called arbitrary power, to make a law to prohibit investigating the principles, good or bad, on which such a law, or any other is founded. If a law be bad, it is one thing to oppose the practice of it, but it is quite a different thing to expose its errors, to reason on its defects, and to show cause why it should be repealed, or why another should be substituted in its place'.

He continues by saying that this is a better course than forcibly violating a bad law.

Freedom of speech, if not Paine's focus, was, however, the central theme of Lord Erskine, England's greatest trial lawyer, when he defended Paine in his absence from England in 1792.[81] His argument turned on Paine's *motives*. It was taken down verbatim at the time and printed the next year, and this extract is often quoted.

'Every man, not intending to mislead, but seeking to enlighten others with what his own reason and conscience, however erroneously, have dictated to him as truth, may address himself to the universal reason of a whole nation, either upon the subject of government in general or on that of our own particular country:—that he may analyse the principles of its constitution,—point out its errors and defects,—examine and publish its corruptions,—warn his fellow citizens against their ruinous consequences,—and exert his whole faculties in pointing out the most advantageous change in establishments which he considers to be radically defective or sliding from their object by use. All this every subject of that country has a right to do, if he

81. Erskine's speech was printed in *The genuine Trial of Thomas Paine for a libel contained in the second part of Rights of Man*; at Guildhall, London, Dec.18, 1792, before Lord Kenyon and a special jury, together with the speeches at large of the Attorney General and Mr Erskine and authentic copies of Mr Paine's letters to the Attorney General and others on the subject of the prosecution, taken in shorthand by E. Hodgson, The second edition corrected, Printed for J. S Jordan, London 1793; Reprinted by Gale Ecco 2010.

contemplates only what he thinks would be for its advantage, and but seeks to change the public mind by the conviction which flows from reasonings dictated by conscience.'

Erskine lost the case, but outside court was met by a crowd which is said to have shouted, 'Damn Tom Paine, but Erskine for ever, and the Liberty of the Press; the King, the Constitution, and Erskine for ever', and to have unhitched his horses and themselves carried Erskine in his carriage to his lodgings.

1.16. KANT IN 1784

Kant spoke of the value of communication in his 'An answer to the question: What is enlightenment?' of 1784. If speaking in an official role under government or the church to the limited audience concerned, one may have temporarily restricted oneself in what one says to serve the ends of one's commonwealth or one's church. But an enlightened monarch in the different role of scholar (*gelehrte*), writing for the whole world, will leave people free to express their thoughts, so long as that is consistent with civil order. That freedom is the least harmful freedom there is. I take this to mean that it is not harmful to civil order, nor in the long run to the commonwealth or church, for neither is currently being addressed. But these institutions may in the long run benefit by evolving towards enlightenment. It is very difficult, Kant says, for individuals to become enlightened. But if a few do so, they may be enough to bring the whole public closer to enlightenment.

1.17. THE CIRCUMVENTION
OF LITERARY CENSORSHIP

Ingenuity has often been required against suppression of speech through the medium of partly hidden satire. Dictatorial regimes in many countries have hesitated to ban Shakespeare productions, or looked ridiculous if they did. A whole issue of *Index on Censorship* has been devoted to this.[82] Favourite Shakespeare plays for staging dissent against one's regime have been those which portray rulers: *Julius Caesar, Richard II, Richard III, Macbeth, King Lear, Hamlet,* or racial differences, *Othello, The Merchant of Venice.*

Shakespeare himself had to contend with censorship by the Master of Revels, Edmund Tilney. In Sonnet 66, he spoke of 'Art, made tongue-tied by authority'. It has been wondered why versions of his play *Richard II* before that of 1601 do not include the scene of the 1601 version, repeated in the 1608 version, in which that king is formally stripped of his crown. Was it added in the 1601 performance in the hope of bolstering the Earl of Essex's unsuccessful plot at that time to depose Queen Elizabeth? The queen herself complained of that later version

---

82. I thank Geoffrey Strachan for introducing me to *Index on Censorship*, 'Staging Shakespearean dissent', *Exact Books*, 24 March 2016, pp. 1–55.

that it was played forty times in the open streets and houses and that she was being identified with Richard II. If so, had Essex encouraged adding the scene in 1601?

It is believed that a fragment of Shakespeare's handwritten contribution has survived to the rewriting of a play *Thomas More*, which was composed by several hands, and marked for cutting. The censor had banned portraying a London riot of 1517 against immigrant workers from Lombardy taking Londoners' jobs, and reflecting arguments contemporary with the play against Huguenot immigrant workers. (I shall come in Chapter 3 to the 2016–2020 campaigns against UK membership of the European Union, with their rhetoric against immigration from Europe). The contribution attributed to Shakespeare shows the late Thomas More, by the time of the play a victim of King Henry VIII's executions, telling the rioters to have feeling for the poor retreating immigrants, and warning that the rioters will in their turn become victims, as fish eat fish. Tilney, however, censored the play in this version too.[83]

In a 1982 production of *Richard III* in Poland, the actor representing Richard's successor, who seized his crown, was required to remove his dark glasses that reminded the audience of their own ruler, General Jaruzelski. In South Africa in 1987, the authorities, who forbade sexual relationships between people of different races, did not dare to ban an embrace between a

---

83. *Index on Censorship*, 2016, articles by Simon Callow, 'Plays, protests and the censor's pencil', at pp. 31–32 and 34–35, and Kathleen E. Mcluskie. 'The play's the thing', at pp. 34–35.

black actor representing Othello and a white actress representing Othello's wife, Desdemona, although the white actress was never allowed to play any part thereafter. A copy of the complete works of Shakespeare was also allowed into the prison library on Robben Island during white rule in South Africa, where the country's imprisoned future leader Nelson Mandela was able to sign his name against this passage of *Julius Caesar*:

> Cowards die many times before their deaths
> The valiant never taste of death but once.
> Of all the wonders that I yet have heard,
> It seems to me most strange that men should fear,
> Seeing that death, a necessary end,
> Will come when it will come.

In India in 2014, the outstanding filmmaker Vishal Bhardwaj had his film *Haider* cleared by the censors, although the film required forty-one cuts. The resulting film transposed Shakespeare's *Hamlet* to Kashmir, where a son, corresponding to Hamlet, goes to look for his murdered father, while his uncle promptly marries his mother. It could be seen just as a beautiful story, or as a striking transposition of *Hamlet*. But it could also be seen as commenting on the role of the Indian army staving off further occupation of Kashmir by infiltrators from Pakistan, but in the process unintentionally turning the bereaved son into a terrorist opponent.

Under Stalin's rule in the Soviet Union from the mid-1920s to his death in 1953, few of the writers and artists he opposed managed to evade censorship, although he praised a small number of those censored, Yevgeny Zamyatin posthumously, and allowed exile to the silenced Vladimir Mayakowski. Zamyatin's last play before his suicide, *We*, used satire, but insufficiently hidden to ward off the condemnation that led him to suicide. However, Mikhail Bulgakov, another writer who was praised but silenced, used hidden satire in his play *Molière*, written in 1929 and banned in 1930. He had named the play after the seventeenth-century playwright whose career had been promoted but then terminated by a parallel relationship with the authoritarian King Louis XIV of France.[84]

The rights to free speech and expression noticed in this overview have often been based on the perceived benefits of such discourse. In the next chapter, we shall find that *voluntary* self-restraint in free speech and expression is sometimes needed if those benefits are to be realized.

84. I thank Geoffrey Strachan for information on the playwrights censored by Stalin.

Chapter 2

The benefits of free speech and expression

Productive versus counter-productive speech, and voluntary boundaries

2.1. THE CASE FOR FREE SPEECH AS ITS VALUE, NOT THE RIGHT TO IT: JOHN STUART MILL, 1859

At the beginning of chapter 1, I gave a negative rationale for free speech: life is so inhumane when it is denied. But, as has already been seen, there is a positive rationale for it as well, connected with its benefits.

When, as we saw in chapter 1, the Fourteenth Amendment to the US Constitution in 1868 introduced to individuals in all the States equal individual *rights* to the 'privileges and immunities' of the first eight Amendments, including free speech, it

Freedom of Speech and Expression. Richard Sorabji, Oxford University Press (2021). © Oxford University Press. DOI: 10.1093/oso/9780197532157.003.0002

was the *rights* that were emphasized. But one of the most comprehensive British cases for freedom of speech, by contrast, was that of John Stuart Mill in *On Liberty*, nine years earlier in 1859, which spoke almost entirely of the *utility* of free speech, not of the individual's *right* to it. Indeed, in paragraph 11 of his Chapter 1, Mill says, 'I forego any advantage that could be derived to my argument from the idea of abstract right as a thing independent of utility'. Most of the utilities he cites are utilities for society. In a civilized community, he thinks, society may restrain an individual's action, only if the action will do *harm* to *others* (Ch. 1, para 9; Ch. 3, para 1). He mentions rights fleetingly when he expands his ban on harming another by saying (Ch. 4, para 3) that one should not injure the *interests* of another in those matters that ought to be considered *rights*. But he sees this as a *return* to society for its benefits, and as a *duty* to *society* by which you are '*bound*', and he does not draw the conclusion that the reason for refraining is the *rights* of the harmed individual. The reference to what *ought* to be considered rights is only to reduce the need to appeal to *legal* enforcement—it is sufficient, he adds, for society to punish hurtful or inconsiderate action by *opinion*.

Somebody might seek to base an individual human right on Mill's point in his Chapter 3, that free speech helps to create individuality, but this was not Mill's conclusion. Mill's case was made notably in Chapter 2 of his *On Liberty* of 1859.[1] In

---

1. I have benefited on Mill and Kant from Onora O'Neill, *Speech Rights, Speech Wrongs*, Van Gorcum, Amsterdam, 2016, pp. 50–51.

Chapter 1, he had defended in the thirteenth paragraph the need for self-expression, subject only to the proviso, which he had made three paragraphs earlier and repeated here, that it should not be allowed to *harm* others. This is later explicated as injuring the *interests* of society,[2] and is not confined to physical harm, as is sometimes claimed. On the other hand, mere offensiveness is allowed. In the second and ninth paragraphs of Chapter 3, he speaks of the value to each individual of developing one's own individuality, though without explicitly offering this as the ground of the need for self-expression. Mill's second chapter is the fullest and here he turns from mere self-expression in abstraction from communication, to communicating with others.

When Mill here turns to communication, he develops Milton's point about *truth*, and argues that hearing the opinions of others, if they are true, enables one to learn, but if they are mistaken, the truth will stand out more clearly. He recommends comparing the opinions of others as an exercise for improving one's own: 'The steady habit of correcting and completing one's own opinion by collating it with those of others, so far from causing doubt and hesitation in carrying it into practice, is the only stable foundation for a just reliance on it'. Further, if it had been made a heresy to question the scientific views of Newton, we would be *less* sure of their truth. Mill thinks it the source of everything to be respected in man that

2. J. S. Mill, *On Liberty*, 1859, Ch. 4, para. 3; Ch. 5, para. 2.

he can correct his mistakes by discussion and experience. He rejects the view that opinions may be useful, whether or not true. He denies the argument that persecution is ineffective in suppressing true belief. The Protestant Reformation broke out twenty times and was put down, before it succeeded under Luther. Even so, free discussion is more effective than persecution at killing mistaken belief. Free discussion is needed for an intellectually active people. Without it, even true opinions are superstition. The Roman orator Cicero rightly saw that to know one's own case, one must study the case of one's adversary. Without discussion, belief is not a living regulator of one's conduct. Nor does one know the full meaning of what one believes. Rival opinions may each have only part of the truth, and Christian belief may need supplementing by non-Christian. Protestants should engage with Catholic views, as likely to contain some portion of the truth.

Some of the concerns we have looked at about restricting free speech have been summarized by the authors of an official Canadian report on accommodating cultural differences within the Canadian Province of Quebec, in a book they based on their report.[3] Who, they ask, has the authority to dictate what speech is allowable and what not? Moreover, restrictions on freedom of speech lead to stagnation. The stagnation of ideas is a concern we have met in both Milton and Mill. Authoritarianism was part of Madison's concern, when

---

3. Jocelyn Maclure and Charles Taylor, *Secularism and Freedom of Conscience*, Harvard University Press, Cambridge, MA, 2011, p. 108.

he started drafting the Amendments to prevent Congress over-riding the individual States.

2.2. MAHATMA GANDHI (1869–1948): OPENING EARS AND THE BENEFITS OF GOOD DISCUSSION

I have elsewhere described Mahatma Gandhi as exemplifying Mill's case for the value of free discussion. I did so partly with reference to a set of seven articles that he wrote in 1926 under the title 'Is this Humanity?'[4] He had praised a municipal council for shooting sixty stray dogs, in case they were carrying rabies. Outraged Hindus wrote in from all over India, saying, 'we thought you were a believer in non-violence'. Gandhi openly published their objections, without caricaturing them, although he allowed himself the wry comment that one of the letters was 'violent', and we see him gradually deepening his conception of non-violence in the course of his articles. He comes to decide that killing is always violent, unless it is carried out for the sake of the killed, as in euthanasia, and that violence is always wrong. Has he not given in,

---

4. They are not available in the 100-volume *Collected Works*, either in the printed or electronic editions, but were translated from Gandhi's Gujarati newspaper *Navajivan* for October to November 1926, for publication in his English newspaper *Young India*. They are translated and recorded with replies to objections by Gandhi's secretary, Mahadev Desai, in his *Day to Day with Gandhi*, vol. 8, Varanasi, 1973, and are discussed in my *Gandhi and the Stoics*, Oxford University Press, Oxford, and Chicago University Press, Chicago, 2012, pp. 85–90.

then, to his critics, as having praised something wrong? Here his discussion takes a still more subtle turn. We have to ask not merely whether it was wrong to shoot the dogs—it was—but also whether it would have been even more wrong not to shoot them. If you serve on the municipal council, you have undertaken to protect the town's citizens, and then it would be *more* wrong not to kill the dogs. Sometimes we are in a moral double-bind: wrong whichever way we act. But we are required to consider which course would be worse. Knowing that the violence is wrong does not tell us what to do. What, then, is the use of such moral principles as that violence is always wrong? The answer, given later, is that it is a counsel of perfection for the imperfect and helps us to raise our sights in the direction of non-violence, even though we cannot always achieve it. Here, by taking objections seriously, Gandhi has come to deeper insights about how to live.

Gandhi had learnt from the Jains what Mill also held, that anyone may have part of the truth. In the Jain version, blind men are holding on to different parts of an elephant, and each has only a very incomplete conception of it, but each is right about the part he is holding. Gandhi adds that the owner will know more, perhaps adverting to the Jain belief in the omniscience of their founder, Mahavira, the most recent of twenty-four divine teachers. However, it is another sign of Gandhi's openness to free discussion that he was not convinced by another Jain belief in which they had been pioneers, non-violence, including non-violence to animals. At least as he understood that non-violence as he found it usually practised in his own time, except by his Jain Guru, Shrimad Rajchandra, the concern not to tread on bugs was a concern with one's own purity, not with the bug's welfare. It did not matter, as he interpreted the Jains, if someone else trod on the bug, and he declares that that view had at first made him a devotee of violence. That was until he read Tolstoy's very different conception of non-violence as an ocean of compassion, when he was converted to a view from a completely different culture and religion.[5] This was only one of many examples of his taking guidance from entirely different directions, while adapting them to fit with his own developing viewpoint.

I think Gandhi's unusual question of 1931 is of great value: 'what opens ears?' But it must be recognized that opening ears is an art. In speaking of opening ears, Gandhi was not, of course, thinking of opening ears by false propaganda to the masses. He was concerned with the ears of his powerful opponents, and with opening ears to *truth*. The name he coined in 1908 for his form of non-violent resistance was *satyagraha*, a firm insistence on truth in oneself and in one's opponent. But he combined this with an insistence on good will towards one's opponent.[6]

Gandhi's opening of ears is illustrated by his Salt March of 1930, in which a huge following of unarmed Indian marchers witnessed the unpredictable culmination of a march of around 220 miles, when Gandhi scooped up salt with his hand from

5. Sorabji, *Gandhi and the Stoics*, pp. 77–78.
6. Sorabji, *Gandhi and the Stoics*, e.g. p. 10

salt pans at the seashore without paying tax in a symbolic violation of a British tax on salt. Though a physical act, this was
also an act of expression. But Gandhi demanded another quality from those followers who took part in civil disobedience, as
opposed to other forms of support. They were never to retali-
ate against British reactions, but to accept whatever retaliation was meted out. At their next visit to the seashore after
Gandhi's arrest, they made no resistance when their members
were struck on the head with iron-tipped staves and fell to the
ground. Gandhi later advised the society he established for
non-political constructive work, the Gandhi Seva Sangh, that
most of its members should not join his political confronta-
tions with the British, because that required being sure that
you could control your temper under retaliation.[7] Gandhi
himself practised self-restraint at a much deeper ascetic level,
including chastity as the hardest discipline, and poverty as a
training in indifference to money.[8] He saw this as a necessary
preparation for adopting non-violence and acceptance of any
punishment that might be encountered.[9] Self-restraint is also

7. Speech to Gandhi Seva Sangh, 21 and 22 February 1940, repr. R. Iyer, ed., *The Moral and Political Writings of Mahatma Gandhi*, vol. 1, Oxford University Press, Oxford, 1986, nos. 149–150, at pp. 415–443.

8. Gandhi, *Indian Home Rule*, English translation, 1910, of Gujarati *Hind Swaraj*, 1909, ed. Anthony J. Parel, *Gandhi, Hind Swaraj and Other Writings*, Cambridge University Press, Cambridge, 1997, pp. 96–98.

9. The earliest statement is in his *Indian Home Rule*, English translation, 1910, of Gujarati *Hind Swaraj*, 1909, ed. Parel, *Gandhi, Hind Swaraj and Other Writings*, pp. 96–98.

one of the qualities needed for sometimes setting aside one's own right to free speech, when its use is counterproductive.

When Gandhi spoke of opening ears, he was thinking of British ears—he was wrong to think that this technique might also have worked with Hitler's. He went on in 1931 to speak of the acceptance of suffering as a tool, something already illustrated by the Salt March of 1919. 'The conviction has been growing on me', he said, 'that things of fundamental importance to the people are not won by reason alone. Suffering is infinitely more powerful than the law of the jungle for converting the opponent and opening his ears, which are otherwise shut, to the voice of reason. [...] The appeal of reason is more to the head but the penetration of the heart comes from suffering. It opens up the inner understanding in man.'[10] Gandhi was advocating a particular form of expression: the acceptance, without complaint or resistance, of any retaliation or punishment meted out by the British in reply to non-violent protest.

According to a recent learned interpretation,[11] the British lost control of India not because of Gandhi, since on this view, the British had already defeated him. It is true that in 1940 he

---

10. Speech at Birmingham meeting, 18 October 1931, *Young India*, 5 November 1931, recorded in electronic *Collected Works*. *The Collected Works of Mahatma Gandhi* (electronic book), Publications Division Government of India, New Delhi, 1999, vol. 54, p. 48 (a different selection from that of the printed edition) https://sites. google.com/site/mahatmagandhionthenet/complete-works.

11. Judith Brown, 'Gandhi and Civil Resistance in India: Key Issues', in Adam Roberts, Timothy Garton Ash, eds., *Civil Resistance and Power Politics: The Experience of Non-violent Action from Gandhi to the Present*, Oxford University Press, Oxford, 2009, pp. 43–57.

left the political base he had dominated, the Indian National Congress, because of its willingness to parley with the British about military conscription to support them in World War II, in return for guaranteed independence afterwards. But I am inclined to think that this leaves out something very important. Gandhi had won international opinion. The surrender of India was not I think the result only of such other factors as British economic impoverishment through the Second World War, but also because Gandhi had before the war won so much sympathy internationally.

A role in opening ears can also be played by *wit*, if it is carefully directed to the right audience. A doctor complained to Gandhi that the faith to which he often appealed was merely unreasonable belief. Why could Gandhi not confine himself to reason? Gandhi replied, 'To take your medicines, doctor, I would need faith'.[12]

2.3. THE CONNECTION OF FREE SPEECH WITH VALUE AND BENEFIT FROM THE GREEKS AND ASHOKA TO JOHN STUART MILL AND GANDHI

I have spoken of Mill and Gandhi as making a case for the good effects of the right kind of speech. But this point can be

---

12. Gandhi, 'Faith vs. reason', *Young India*, 14 April 1927.

generalized by recalling the connection of free speech with value and benefit, in the examples already given in chapter 1 from the Greeks onwards. The Athenian democracy surely allowed equal speech (*isēgoria*) to their citizens in the political assembly partly in order to secure the best decisions. It encouraged its comic poets in ridiculing those who had become too prominent in politics, in the spirit of discouraging a turn to authoritarianism. The Cynic philosophers in Athens, we saw in chapter 1, were allowed free speech, with Diogenes replying to his admirer Alexander the Great, 'Stand out of my light'. The Cynics were later said, however, to have earned their right to irreverence by their helpfulness, for example in terminating quarrels. Ashoka stressed the benefits of different religious persuasions listening to each other, rather than casting out the unpopular persuasions. Akbar the Great thought that fellow-Muslims among his Indian subjects would benefit from translation of the different views of Hinduism. In the period of English civil wars in the 1640s, Milton saw the right to publication without prior license as a benefit. In 1784, Kant thought that leaving people free to express their thoughts, if consistent with civil order, could have the benefit of bringing the public closer to enlightenment. In the period from 1789 to 1792, the French revolutionaries surely saw freedom of speech as something good in itself for the society they hoped to create. In 1789, Madison, in the first draft of his First Amendment to the US Constitution (fourth point), saw free speech as a great bulwark of liberty. In 1791–1792, Thomas Paine, in *The Rights of Man*, argued for the freedom to expose bad law by consideration of basic principles, and replace it by good law. His legal defender, Lord Erskine, backed Paine's right to engage in this activity, provided he was seeking his country's advantage.

Mill too, in his *On Liberty* of 1859, associates free speech with the value of its benefits, as can be seen by looking at the benefits he picks out. In celebrating the following first seven benefits, he is conscious that they would often be lost if speech were not free.

(1) *Truth.* Mill has a fuller account than Milton of how freedom of speech is necessary for finding truth, since that depends on discussion.

(2) It also gives us more confidence about *finding* the truth—we would not have confidence in Newton's theories, if it was forbidden to question them.

(3) *Understanding our own case.* Mill refers to Cicero as lawyer, and interprets him as thinking that we do not know even our own case, until we understand our opponent's.

(4) Free speech makes an *intellectually active*, instead of a *superstitious*, people.

(5) Without free discussion, one does not know the *full meaning* of what one believes.

(6) It enables your beliefs to *regulate your conduct*.

(7) Each person has only *part of the truth*, so one needs to share, as the Jain faith in India also holds.

These benefits are surveyed in Chapter 2 of *On Liberty*, and they all involve comparing and contrasting ideas. Although this is Mill's main subject, we saw that his Chapter 1 discusses self-expression, and his Chapter 3 mentions, without drawing a conclusion, that

(8)   self-expression helps us to *create our individuality*. But self-expression is not being thought of as private soliloquy, even if one starts by thinking out privately how to express oneself in public. So public exchange is still under consideration.

2.4. MILL'S SUCCESSORS

Others too since Mill have highlighted one or another different benefits provided by free speech, and recognized their being dependent on our freedom to speak. Timothy Garton Ash[13] agrees with Mill that free speech helps one to find the truth and adds that it helps one to

(9)   create one's identity, but by enabling one to *find out what to think, and so to believe this rather than that*. It is also important for

13. Timothy Garton Ash, *Free Speech*, Atlantic Books, London, 2016, pp. 73–79. There is a good discussion also in a book concerned with Indian practice, Gautam Bhatia, *Offend, Shock, or Disturb*, Oxford University Press, Delhi, 2016, pp. 4–24.

(10) *autonomy* that one should be able to judge for oneself what to believe and how to act, and this depends on people being able to speak freely. On a public scale, Garton Ash adds, freedom of speech allows for

(11) a more *responsive government* within one's own territory, especially within a democracy, because it allows government to hear what people want and what are the good and bad effects of its policies. Even under colonial rule, free speech by a man like Gandhi can influence government.

All recent authors, unlike Mill, are very conscious of the tradition stemming from the First Amendment to the US Constitution. Among the retrospective philosophical rationales added since the Fourteenth Amendment for the individual's right to free speech in a democracy, Alexander Meiklejohn stressed that free speech provides

(12) *the information necessary for citizens in a democracy to carry out their political responsibilities as citizens.*[14] Thomas Scanlon, in his revision of an earlier rationale of his, thought that Meiklejohn should have added that free speech offers

(13) *to citizens the right to advocate their own interests and point of view.*[15] I mentioned in chapter 1 that a sense

14. Alexander Meiklejohn, *Political Freedom*, Oxford University Press, Oxford, 1960.
15. T. M. Scanlon Jr., 'Freedom of expression and categories of expression', *University of Pittsburg Law Review* 40, 1979, pp. 519–550, at 530.

of having any voice in politics can sink to a low ebb at times of divided national opinion.

I am less clear that freedom of speech necessarily

(14) *helps one live with diversity*, as Timothy Garton Ash has said,[16] *or encourages tolerance*, as Raphael Cohen-Almagor ascribes to a number of authors,[17] rather than providing a difficult challenge to tolerance, which may be met more or less well.

Cohen-Almagor also cites the view that free speech is

(15) *central to human dignity.*

Stanley Fish has listed several further reasons that have been given for saying that free speech is essential to democracy.[18] It is essential because it promotes the free flow of ideas and so provides

(16) *citizens (and it might be added, politicians) capable of independent judgement.* Moreover, citizens should be encouraged to dissent, in order

16. Garton Ash, *Free Speech*, pp. 73–79.
17. Raphael Cohen-Almagor, 'J. S. Mill's boundaries of freedom of expression: a critique', *Philosophy* 92, 2017, pp. 565–596, at 566–567.
18. Stanley Fish, 'The dance of theory', in Lee C. Bollinger and Geoffrey R. Stone, eds., *Eternally Vigilant: Free Speech in the Modern Era*, University of Chicago Press, Chicago, 2002, p. 200.

(17) to *check state power*, to which Michael Sandel adds
Madison's bugbear, the *tyranny of the majority*.[19]

2.5. WHAT TYPES OF DISCUSSION DO THESE BENEFITS REQUIRE, AND WHAT OUTCOMES FROM DISCUSSION?

Many of the benefits cited depend in some way on discussion, although self-expression may begin with private thought. But what sort of discussion is required? Mill and others envisage discussion with people of *opposing* views. So the kind of echo chamber (or 'filter bubble') discussion, which will be explored in chapter 3, would be the very *opposite* of what is wanted. For in that scenario, social media platforms filter to groups of people only the information they would *like* to hear. That way, they become popular sites for people to visit and so, like popular newspapers but on a vaster scale, attract advertising revenue. They ascertain personal preferences from information voluntarily offered to chat platforms, or acquired through the use of 'cookies' which collect personal information as the price for allowing access to websites, or through monitoring the use of i-phones, which yields much more personal information again. People with similar preferences are then put into groups by the use of algorithms and are fed only selected information which fits their preferences.

19. Sandel, *Democracy's Discontent*, p. 43.

Mill and others, by contrast, envisage a discussion in which the opponents, so far from confirming your opinions, put the opposite side of the case. This connects with Mill's interest in finding the truth, an interest he takes over from Milton. Of course, presentation of a rival case may not happen.[20] Some opponents may be silent, or may rant abusively, or, even worse, may try to shout you down. They then lose their chance of learning anything from you, and you too will be able to learn very little, if anything, from them, so that the valued purpose of discussion is not fulfilled.

On the other hand, benefit does not depend on *agreement* being reached. In neither Milton nor Mill, nor before them in Akbar, was converting the other side part of the purpose. Akbar had been positively against conversion; he wanted Muslims, and if possible Hindus, to correct their own mistakes through access to the opposed view. The previous emphasis in Mill was repeatedly about improving your *own* view in various ways. Not only can you learn parts of the truth previously unappreciated, but with free discussion you can gain confidence in finding the truth, better see what your own case should be, know the full meaning of what you believe, have it regulate your conduct, and become more intellectually active and further from superstition. In political discussions, again the desired effect typically concerns oneself. With improved ability to judge independently, you can judge better what to believe and how to

---

20. I am grateful to Steven Birnbaum and Alex Guerrero for drawing my attention to cases of this and for further discussion.

act. You can hear the political information you need to act on. These benefits do not include convincing the opposite party. As regards convincing the government, less can be expected. Government can at least hear what you advocate, although it may not be persuaded. It is not suggested that any one individual can often check state power, although it is not impossible that enough people banded together might.

Speech is thought of in most of these contexts as aimed at ascertaining the truth. But of course there are acts of speech and expression with a different aim. I have discussed earlier Mahatma Gandhi's seven articles investigating when killing could be seen as non-violent.[21] This discussion with opponents was aimed at working out the truth. But Gandhi's expressive act, at the end of his Salt March in 1930, of scooping up a handful of sea salt without paying the British salt tax, was aimed at a *rescinding* of the British salt tax.

Mill underestimated the projects of the ruler Akbar in intercultural reading, when he treated him as a ruler who wanted to improve a barbarian people who were not yet capable of being improved by free and equal discussion. Given that, Mill concluded, Akbar was entitled to rely on despotism for creating improvement.[22] Akbar himself, however, we saw in chapter 1, commissioned adaptations from Sanskrit into Persian of the

---

21. Gandhi, 'Is this humanity?' translated from Gandhi's newspaper *Navajivan*, Oct–Nov 1926, by his secretary, Mahadev Desai, in the latter's *Day to Day with Gandhi*, vol. 8, discussed in Sorabji, *Gandhi and the Stoics*, pp. 85–93.
22. Mill, *On Liberty*, Ch. 1, para. 10.

two greatest Hindu religious epics, with the aim, according to the adapter's preface, of enabling his Muslim subjects to get rid of some of their mistakes by reading or hearing a Persianized version of a different religion's beliefs.

2.6. USE OF OUR RIGHT TO FREE SPEECH IS COUNTERPRODUCTIVE, IF IT FRUSTRATES THE BENEFITS AND THE MEANS TO ACQUIRE THEM

So much for the widely recognized benefits of free speech, and we are very fortunate if speech with these benefits is guaranteed to us. But what about speech that frustrates the benefits cited? The benefits for which freedom of speech is rightly valued suggest a method for identifying boundaries on free speech that should appeal to the very protagonists who recognize these major benefits, as I do myself. Free speech should indeed be cherished when it brings us these goods. But speech sailing under false colours of securing these benefits, while actually impeding them, should not be allowed to share the presumption in its favour. This is not to say how it should be treated when it impedes these values, because finding the right remedy for such serious damage is a difficult question. But when free speech actually impedes the normal benefits, it should at once surrender the prestige earned by that freedom of speech which really does provide these goods. My main examples in this chapter will concern religious abuse, and in chapter 3, I will focus on other kinds of abuse. But first I will mention a few topical examples of free speech apparently frustrating its benefits.

2.7. PRELIMINARY EXAMPLES OF FREE SPEECH RISKING FRUSTRATION OF ITS INTENDED BENEFITS

One example has just been mentioned. Suppose one group exercises free speech by shouting down the free speech of another group; then neither group can reap the intended benefits of free speech.[23] Other examples are currently topical. In the stormy year of 2016, there were voting campaigns in both Britain and the United States. In the United States, the question was raised whether a presidential candidate, Donald Trump, had encouraged gun owners to shoot his rival for the presidency, by saying that *only* gun owners could forestall the liberal proposals of his rival. Given that any resulting danger to his rival was not clear and present (immediate), it was therefore not illegal by the criteria that I shall discuss in chapter 3. But if any threat was intended, it would be a relevant question whether such an act of free speech frustrated, instead of enhancing, the whole idea of democratic

---

23. I thank Steven Birnbaum for the example.

elections. There was also a question about a reported threat by the same candidate to deport all Muslims from the country. If there was such a threat, the question arises whether that frustrated the ideals of unity and equality (which affect speech) in a democratic nation. A question about a political death threat arose also in the United Kingdom. There a man was prosecuted for inciting motorists to run their cars over Gina Miller, the private citizen who went to the Supreme Court in 2016 and successfully challenged the right of government ministers to bypass Parliament in initiating a constitutional change affecting British citizens, namely Britain's exit from the European Union, or 'Brexit'. This was in the context of a divisive UK referendum of 2016 and its aftermath, which raised questions just as severe as any raised in the United States. To take a final US example, free speech was also involved in the US Supreme Court decision of January 2010 to treat the political campaign donations of large corporations or their owners as free speech,[24] and then by 5 to 4 in 2014 to strike down the previous limit on their total donation, by allowing them to support as many candidates or committees as they liked.[25] The objectors complained that counting this as free speech removed the benefit of equality of opportunity for ordinary citizens to make their own speech count in democratic elections.

24. Warren Richie, *Christian Science Monitor*, 21 January 2010.
25. Dan Roberts in *The Guardian*, 2 April 2014.

2.8. ABUSE OF RELIGIONS INSIDE AND OUTSIDE ONE'S JURISDICTION

The cases which I shall here take as the main example of free speech which frustrates the benefits for which free speech is valued are certain cases of religious abuse.[26] To take the United States first, in 2011 and 2012, a Christian pastor in Florida burnt copies of the Muslim holy book, the Koran, and tried to burn nearly 3,000 copies in 2013, but was prevented. Again in an attack on Islam, an amateur movie made in the United States in 2011 presented the Prophet as killing a pregnant woman, engaging in heterosexual activity with different women, with a question raised about homosexuality, and preparing to attack all infidels. Some scenes were obtained illegitimately by deceiving the actors about the identity of Prophet as the central character portrayed. The movie was posted as a video on YouTube in 2012 and triggered dozens of protests from northwest Africa to southeast Asia, including violent protests at American embassies in Tunis, Khartoum, Cairo, Sana, and Jakarta. Fifty people were killed in protests all over the world, including Pakistan, Afghanistan, Europe, India, Africa, and Australia. Twenty-one governments asked YouTube to block or review the movie.

In Europe, the denigrations had started earlier. In 2005, the Danish newspaper *Jyllands-Posten* published twelve cartoons,

---

26. I take the following examples from Garton Ash, *Free Speech*, Atlantic Books, London 2016, pp. 62–72, 143–147.

some portraying the Prophet. Mere portrayal is itself contrary to quite widespread, but not universal, Islamic sentiment. But more serious was the cartoon by a member of the newspaper's staff portraying the Prophet as a terrorist with a bomb lit in his turban and the Islamic Creed written on the bomb. This required no courage, for the producers of the cartoons were not themselves at the time subject to any personal danger, although protests elsewhere in Muslim countries later led to a large number of deaths of other people. The cartoons could not claim the value of artistic merit or good humour.

The Danish newspaper which published the 2005 cartoons claimed to be defending Western civilization. Moreover, it was reported[27] that the paper showed double standards by refusing to print cartoons ridiculing Jesus, because they might offend some Christians. It has been argued[28] that some of the Muslim reactions to the cartoons went back to wounded feelings in 1989 over the treatment of the Prophet in Salman Rushdie's novel of 1988, *The Satanic Verses*. Rushdie there entered the new realm of theological satire, with political consequences. The death sentence pronounced on him by an Iranian Ayatollah for apostasy from the Muslim faith was a political command, a *hakam*, I am told.[29] There is no doubt that Muslims were wounded by the novel, but a death

---

27. By G. Fouché, *The Guardian*, 6 February 2006.
28. Faisal Devji, *The Terrorist in Search of Humanity*, Hurst, London, 2008, Ch. 6, 'Insulting the Prophet', pp. 165–200.
29. By Faisal Devji.

sentence pronounced by a foreign jurisdiction on a writer in England for change of religious adherence, and addressed to anyone who could carry it out, was no more likely than Western reactions to allow for discussion between the parties, much less to open ears. It is possible that the Danish 'defence of Western civilization' was also a reference back to the death sentence.

In 2006, The French satirical weekly *Charlie Hebdo* reprinted the Danish cartoons. In 2011, its offices were fire-bombed after it printed a rather crude further cartoon of the Prophet, but on the other hand presenting him as encouraging laughter at certain social practices ascribed to Islam, for which blame was placed on Muslims *other* than the Prophet. In 2012, it published a further series of cartoons of the Prophet, including nude caricatures. In 2015, two gunmen entered the headquarters of *Charlie Hebdo* in Paris and killed twelve people, including the publishing director Charb, cartoonists, and editors. This was a horrifying murder and naturally the leaders of Europe assembled in Paris to display their solidarity. But though solidarity was called for, it further impeded the opening of ears. In Niger many churches were burnt and people killed and there were violent demonstration with shooting in Pakistan. There was a better response in the Chechen Republic, where a demonstration estimated to have included up to a million people protested against the depictions of the Prophet, but declared Islam to be a religion of peace, not violence, and the Chechen leader declared a public holiday and denounced people without spiritual or moral values.

The attacks on Islam[30] and reactions to them present a test case for questions of freedom of speech or expression. Does burning the Koran in Florida, or denigrating the Prophet by cartoon, or by video, support or impede the goods we hope for from freedom of speech and expression? Surely, it stopped the discussion that most mattered, that between non-Muslims and Muslims. It stopped it not only in the country of the denigrator, but with the 1.6 billion Muslims across the world, currently 23% of the world's population, second in numbers only to Christianity.[31] It thus impeded the very benefits that make free speech and expression so valuable. It impeded what Mill valued, the *recognition of the truth* about oneself and the other, and the *understanding* of one's own case through understanding the other's. That is not for one moment to allow that murder was a justifiable response to the earlier provocations. On the contrary, it was unjustifiable both in itself and because it too, like the attacks on the Prophet, closed off free discussion and understanding. It closed off understanding of what could have motivated the cartoons, or of why other people might kill in return; it put an end to discussion. It called for solidarity with those who had suffered the loss inflicted by the killings. Solidarity was essential, even though solidarity itself is with one side and further prevents the discussion that there might have been with the other side. My complaint is not against the

---

30. I count these as attacks on Islam, even though I agree with Fara Dabhoiwala's comment to me that attackers may often be seeking first to impress their own circle, and would have no interest in Mill's benefits.

31. Figures from the pie chart in Garton Ash, *Free Speech*, 2016, p. 258.

solidarity, but against the decisions to caricature the Prophet and then to reissue the caricatures, decisions which put us in a situation whose consequences further closed discussion with the original party. The decisions to engage in these speech acts set off a chain of effects which impeded Westerners from judging Islam for themselves, cut off communication with Muslims, and, vice versa, prevented Muslims judging Westerners and communicating, producing defensive and closed minds on both sides. All surely greatly reduced the likelihood of being able to live together in tolerance.

I shall come to a better French tradition of cartooning in a moment. But first, did these acts allow other goods to flourish, by fostering the goal of everyone feeling they had a say in a nation's politics, or permitting the government concerned to become more responsive to people within their jurisdiction? But there was not one jurisdiction, only two sides. The attacks on the Prophet were directed at least as much against Muslims in *other* countries outside the home jurisdiction. In that connection, all the arguments about free speech strengthening democracy in the country where the speech was produced drop away as irrelevant. Nor is it likely to have made good government easier in the home country. I do not know the effect on all the loyal French Muslims who, though offended by the cartoons, were nonetheless horrified by the murders, and whether it has made them feel themselves beleaguered objects of suspicion. But certainly that effect has been produced by this and other episodes in England. After what happened, for one side to speak of freedom of speech risks giving freedom of speech a bad name. In the same way, if there had been Muslim complaints of blasphemy from the other side, this could have hardened objections among many to the very concept of blasphemy, although it has been argued that complaints of blasphemy were not the Muslim reaction. It is enough to say that we should consider whether continuing insistence on free speech as a right harms the very values that we believe free speech can serve.

This is not to deny that free speech is a right. It is endorsed as a right by Article 19 of the 1948 United Nations Declaration of Human Rights and by Article 10 of the European Convention on Human Rights of 1953. In some cases it is a right based on human nature. East Germany was violating the human need for and right to family, friendship, and interest groups when it had everybody spied on. This should be prohibited by law and is prohibited by privacy laws. But the rights provided for free speech should not be allowed to obscure the question of how to produce the good effects for which it is valued.

The French had an excellent tradition of cartoons directed against their own government from 1915 in the *Le Canard Enchainé*.[32] This weekly called for courage and skilful investigation in its attempted exposures, sometimes controversial, of wrongdoing at home. The nearest present equivalent in England is perhaps *Private Eye*. In eighteenth-century England, the political cartoons of Gillray were particularly savage, once again against rulers at home, and to this day, cartoons surely

---

32. I thank Nicholas Bayne for reminding me of this.

often help to identify and encapsulate undesirable political—or religious—behaviour, and keep a *check on the home country's government, or élites*. They can also check the might of *an occupying power*. They can represent beacons of *autonomy*, and they may sometimes be able to strike a chord in a separate culture. But not every use of autonomy is equally good, and it can be very sinister. It has been said[33] that historians of the Nazi Third Reich in Germany agree that caricatures of Jews in *Stürmer* played a role in their dehumanization, a dehumanization without which the Holocaust or genocide could not have happened. It was further argued by an Israeli in 1974 that the American cartoon of a hook-nosed Arab holding the world in his claws was entirely similar, when it was used in protest the day after the price rise in petrol then agreed by the Arab countries. In 2005–2006 and 2012, the cartoonists were not promoting the benefits of free speech by making good home government easier, or by striking a chord in the minds of their targets.

2.9. A MODEST PROPOSAL FOR VOLUNTARY BOUNDARIES ON FREE SPEECH

I started chapter 2 by looking for boundaries on free speech that should appeal to the very protagonists who recognize the

---

33. I am grateful to Marwan Rashed for drawing my attention to Ilan Halevi, 'Vers une guerre des civilisations? L'affaire des caricatures du Prophète', in *Du souvenir, du mensonge et de l'oubli. Chroniques palestiniennes*, Paris, *Éditions Actes Sud*, 2016, pp. 227–241, published online by Médecins Sans Frontières.

major benefits it brings. I can now make a modest proposal about such boundaries. If some free speech impedes the very values it is meant to serve, does that not provide all protagonists of free speech, myself included, with a boundary line conforming to our own values? One area, I am suggesting, in which free speech may be thought to frustrate its own good purposes is the case in which it is used to denigrate religious feeling in such a way as to bring to an end discussion with the religion attacked. In advocating free speech, should not exceptions be made and discussion-stopping speech be marked off as not normally[34] deserving the approbation given to other free speech? Protagonists would secure all they value in free speech, while making clear that they will neither celebrate, nor practise such discussion-stopping speech themselves. The US president Bill Clinton did indeed call the cartoons appalling. Withholding support and practice should be voluntary, and not the effect of a law forbidding advocacy or practice. It will be helped if opinion makers, like Bill Clinton at the time, lead the way.

2.10. USING DIFFERENT MODES OF EXPRESSION TO 'OPEN EARS'

But if this is right, it is necessary to think further. For after an act of discussion-stopping speech, it is not enough to withhold

---

34. I say 'normally' because a considered declaration of war, for example, may occasionally be a courageous decision to end discussion.

support from such speech. A next step would be to try another form of speech or expression. For that, I think Gandhi's concept of opening ears is of great value. But it must be recognized that opening ears is an art. There have in effect been millennia of advice on opening ears, some of it illustrated in the previous discussion. We saw one way of opening ears, when the Indian emperor Ashoka in the third century BCE presented his edicts about free speech not as commands, but as his desires. And we saw another in Akbar's encouragement to look at what might be good or bad equally in one's own and in rival published views.[35]

Different modes of speech were also handled in ancient Greek philosophy in the context of teaching. It is not always noticed that Plato in the fourth century BCE shows, without ever saying it, that Socrates did not cure his opponents Thrasymachus and Callicles of their aggressive support for injustice by refuting them.[36] Instead, refutation made them even more aggressive and angry and broke off discussion. Socrates' profitable discussions involved refuting friends and making them *want* to think again.

The degree of frankness of speech can also make a difference. From the different context of the residential philosophy

---

35. This is not the same as the system of exposition followed in Indian philosophy called *purva paksha*, in which the opponent's views have first to be carefully explained, and then refuted, before one puts one's own view, in order that one's own view may be seen to avoid the objections. That may be compared rather with Aristotle's method of first surveying received opinions (*endoxa*), in order to show contradictions in them, and thus reach his own view which preserves *some* of received opinion, while avoiding the contradictions. Both approaches are critical in intent, even while making concessions.

36. Plato, *Republic* Book I, *Gorgias*, from 481B.

school of Epicurus in Athens, a text survives, *On Frank Criticism* (*parrhēsia*),[37] by a later Epicurean, Philodemus. Describing the school's practices at the time of his teacher, Zeno of Tarsus, in the second century BCE, Philodemus treats achieving the right degree of frankness as an art. The students, and even the teachers, had to start the day by making confessions of their deviations from Epicurean practice, and the overseeing of confessions involved a very different use of free (or frank) speech. Criticism was seen as an art to be tailored in frankness to the different characters of different students. One fragment, 67, on the standard reading, says that if the professor quickly turns away from assisting the student who is slipping up, the student's swelling (*sunoidēsis*) will subside. Why should professorial neglect make a *swelling* subside? This makes no sense, and an emendation suggested a long time ago by C. J. Vooys should be accepted. *Suneidēsis* (conscience) differs from *sunoidēsis* (swelling) by only the one letter 'e', which in Greek, as in English, looks very like an 'o', so that the words are easily confused. Moreover, four lines later the related verb appears, *suneidenai*, to recognize in one's conscience. It makes perfect sense that the student's conscience will become less intense if the professor does not offer criticism and help of the right sort. Here *parrhēsia* does not involve risky liberties, but art is

---

37. Philodemus, *On Frank Criticism*, with Greek and translation by David Konstan, Diskin Clay, Clarence E. Glad, Johan C. Thorn, and James Ware, Scholars Press, Atlanta, GA, 1988.

required for gauging the right degree of frankness of speech for the individual.[38] The Epicureans were right that different degrees of frankness are needed and that finding the right degree is an art.

At the level of *self*-expression, two Stoics practised self-restraint in seeking to preserve their own chosen identities, rather than expressing any animosity towards others. Epictetus, the Stoic ex-slave, exiled by the emperor Domitian in the first century CE, said without bitterness that the person who treats you ill, or speaks ill of you, is following his own viewpoint; he cannot follow yours. Later in the same century, the Stoic emperor Marcus Aurelius responded without aggression in relation to those who sinned against him or were untrustworthy, or ungrateful, by reflecting that either they couldn't know any better, or at any rate they were, as fellow humans, his kin.[39]

We saw in chapter 1 that the Greek philosopher and civil servant Themistius in the fourth century CE praised the true Cynic philosopher, who, before criticizing others, must first humbly examine himself: ('am I too one such?') and even after that, must rebuke only in order to cure. Further, he must adjust severity and humility to the character of the person addressed,

---

38. Richard Sorabji, *Moral Conscience through the Ages*, Oxford University Press and Chicago University Press, Oxford and Chicago, 2014, p. 25.
39. Marcus Aurelius, *Meditations*, not know better: 7.26; 8,14; 9,42; 11,18.2; akin: 2.1. The first reason previously in Epictetus *Handbook* 42.

just as had been recommended earlier by the Epicurean Philodemus, and must leave behind concord.[40] It is important not to make the mistake reported later in the Neoplatonist school at Athens, where Damascius was to record his mentor Isidore accusing a pupil of Proclus. Isidore said of the religious enthusiast Hegias, 'Those who are going to be gods must first become human'.[41] This criticism fits with a recent portrait of Proclus himself as so obsessed with his own relation to the gods that he did not notice the off-putting effect on his human associates in the Neoplatonist school which he ran for nearly fifty years in the fifth century CE.[42]

I think it is true even in debates on subjects of purely academic interest that aggressive speech tends to produce defensiveness. Time is wasted while the addressee seeks ever more ingenious arguments for earlier assertions, long after anyone is likely to be converted. By contrast, a receptive and friendly questioning can even lead to a confession that the addressees are not so sure about their beliefs. That can lead to cooperative discussion about what was true and what untrue in the original position offered.

40. Themistius, *On Virtue*, 51–52, tr. Albert Rigolio, *Ancient Commentators on Aristotle*, Bloomsbury, London, 2019.
41. Damascius, *The Philosophical History*, ed. Polymnia Athanassiadi, Apamea Cultural Association, Athens, 1999, 150.
42. Christian Wildberg, 'Proclus of Athens: A Life', in Pieter D'Hoine, Marije Martijn, eds., *All from One: A Guide to Proclus*, Oxford University Press, Oxford, 2016, Ch. 1, pp. 1–26.

2.11. UNDERSTANDING THE OPPONENT'S CASE: ST PAUL AND HOW TO OPPOSE BLASPHEMY CHARGES IN ONE'S OPPONENT'S TERMS

One of Mill's most important contributions was his conclusion, extrapolated from Cicero, that you do not know your own case until you know your opponent's. For example, in opposing blasphemy laws, it would be desirable to understand the position of those who bring charges of blasphemy. This can be understood by those who do not themselves believe in the God of the Abrahamic religions. What is needed is not belief, but imaginative understanding. One reason why blasphemy is significant may be that to denigrate or belittle the one on whom your very being and that of the whole universe is believed to depend is incomparably heinous. In fact, one reason why I am very much against anti-blasphemy laws is that, from the point of view of believers, the crime is so heinous as to demand punishment in excess of any that should be entrusted to humans. But if this is what makes blasphemy heinous, it is important to understand, and not to ignore, the reason for its significance in jurisdictions (unlike the UK) where blasphemy law is enforced. Understanding the reason, I suggested earlier, need not in any way put an end to discussion. In fact, the Christian Paul, though understanding the significance of blasphemy, had a canny answer, when he said, 'It is written: "Vengeance is mine; I will repay," saith the Lord' (Romans 12:19). He was here citing the Old Testament (Deuteronomy 32:35), in which the writer presents a jealous and vengeful God, forbidding the worship of false gods: 'Vengeance is mine, and recompense, for the time when their foot shall slip; for the day of their calamity is at hand, and their doom comes swiftly.' But Paul is using the quotation for his own very different purpose of saying, 'avenge not yourselves'. His use of the quotation provides a reply that could be understood by anyone calling for human vengeance for blasphemy. Thereby he met the requirement extrapolated from Cicero by Mill, that in order to know your own case, you must know your opponent's opposite case. Paul shows that refraining from abusive vengeance does not stop one producing a non-abusive argument that the other side can appreciate. The case against human vengeance need not depend on sharing belief in a vengeful God. It can be taken instead as putting to believers the question, 'Who are we to assess the right response to such a thing? Are we not usurping God's role?' This recognition of the opposing opinion could open ears.

An alternative approach that has, incorrectly I think, been ascribed to Robert Post, could not succeed. By this approach, a rationale for blasphemy law that no thinking believer would accept has been imputed to them, in the claim that 'The original idea of blasphemy law was to protect God, or at least the respect due to God'. The first of these attributions is then easily ridiculed: an almighty God needs no protection from humans. But in fact, it is only the second idea, the respect properly due to God, that is canvassed by Post in the article cited.[43] He paraphrases Blackstone's idea of 1769, 'prevent disrespect to God' as 'protecting the respect due to God', and paraphrases more recent blasphemy laws as 'protect[ing] the sacred by enforcing the respect due to God' (pp. 76–77). By that Post did not mean, I think, protecting God as sacred, but preserving the right *human* attitudes to the sacred.

Looking into actual reasons why the cartoons of the Prophet caused offence, we need not assume that blasphemy was necessarily the point of contention. But there is the same need to understand another's view, without necessarily sharing it. We need to understand why 78% of *British* Muslims interviewed found the cartoons of the Prophet deeply offensive to them personally, which is not for a moment to say that any such proportion believed in taking vengeance. They are more likely to have felt beleaguered, the opposite of the effect good government should produce. The more the attitude of believers is understood—it does not need to be shared—the better, because otherwise non-believers are talking only to those who share their own view. Understanding is also better for living together in a country, and in the world, given that a present estimate is that Christians and Muslims constitute 55% of the world's population, and religious adherence 84%.[44]

43. Robert C. Post, 'Religion and freedom of speech: Portraits of Muhammad', *Constellations* 14, 2007, pp. 72–90, repr. in Andráa Sajó, *Censorial Sensitivities*, Eleven International, Utrecht, 2007, is cited in Garton Ash, *Free Speech*, note 48 to p. 267.
44. The reaction of British Muslims is reported by Garton Ash, *Free Speech*, p. 146, and estimated world figures for religion by the pie chart on p. 258.

Some of the objections raised against one or another boundary to free speech appear to miss the points just made. The 'assassin's veto' argument deplores refraining from abuse if that is based simply on fear of some people being assassinated. But that ignores the reason I am recommending for voluntarily refraining from abuse. The reason is the desirability of understanding the other's view sufficiently to see why offence is being taken, and in the light of that, considering also whether exercising one's right will further or frustrate the benefits of free speech. Horror at assassination is justified, but it coincides with this further reason for voluntarily refraining from abuse.

2.12. OTHER EXAMPLES OF UNDERSTANDING THE OTHER'S CASE

There are other examples in which it is more helpful to learn from, than to abuse, the other's position. Philoponus, the sixth-century CE Greek commentator on Aristotle, though a Christian, was steeped in pagan philosophy, and thought there was good reason for his Christian students to study the logic of the pagan Aristotle. At least, I have argued elsewhere that Philoponus's lectures are the ultimate source of a text mentioned earlier in chapter 1, the preface to an introduction to Aristotle's logic, presented to Khushru I of Persia, king from 531 to 578 CE, by one of the king's subjects, Paul the Persian.[45] The original lecture, probably heard by Paul the Persian, will have pointed out that there are opposing views about religious matters, and in the absence of demonstrative proof, one must resort to faith or understanding. But it is difficult for faith to decide between opposing views. Moreover, the text continues, that other Paul, Christ's Apostle himself, implies in his Epistle 1 to the Corinthians, 13:12, that there is something better than faith, when he says, 'Now we see through a glass darkly, but then we shall see face to face'. We cannot yet see God face to face, but we can help our faith, which is about distant things, by understanding, which is about things close to us (the concepts in our minds). The implication is that Aristotle's logic will help faith to decide among opposing views on religious matters, until such time as God can be seen face to face.

Philoponus's potential students would have shared his belief in there being something beyond 'through a glass darkly'. But sometimes in philosophy and elsewhere it can be a service to show other people what they should or could believe to be the truth given what *they*, not you, believe to be the truth. This can be a service, if you do not pretend to believe and the motivation is good. For example, the theory of evolution of species,

45. Richard Sorabji, 'The cross-cultural spread of Greek philosophy (and Indian moral tales) to 6th century Persian and Syriac', *Studia Graeco-Arabica* 19, 2019, pp. 147–163. The main text in question here, lost in Greek, but preserved in Syriac with a nineteenth-century Latin translation, is given by J. P. N. Land, *Anecdota Syriaca*, vol. 4, 1855, online in http://dbooks.bodleian.ox.ac.uk/books/PDFs/555081467.pdf with the preface in Latin at vol. 4, pp. 1–5 = pp. 408–412 online.

or of the universe, is incompatible with the simple idea that God created everything, as it now is, at the beginning. But this is not the only Christian theory of creation. There are alternative views which should be known: in the fifth century CE, the great Christian thinker, Augustine, held that what God created at the beginning was something like the immaterial patterns in seeds which develop later.[46] The value of this idea, though not Augustine's interest, is that believers need not quarrel with the teaching of evolution, if that evolution can be seen as programmed by God into the original seeds of humans in coordination with the evolving seeds in the environment. As with blasphemy, abuse is again not required and discussion need not stop. Richard Dawkins, today's most prominent opponent of creationism, has been like Akbar to the extent of opposing the idea that the world was recently created, but in his hostility to his Creationist opponents, he did not use Akbar's method of opening people's ears.

In my own family well over a century ago, Cornelia Sorabji entered into the beliefs of secluded Indian women of a certain wealthy class, to protect them from disadvantageous practices. They were often child wives or widows denied a school education. For recovery from a difficult childbirth, she reminded one family that, instead of a pan of fiery hot coals on the mother's stomach, they should recall their belief that Ganges water as

---

46. Detailed in Richard Sorabji, *Time, Creation and the Continuum*, Duckworth, London, 1983; Chicago University Press, Chicago, 2006; Bloomsbury, London, 2013, pp. 302–305.

well as fire was holy. A container of Ganges water pre-heated by coals would be a doubly holy remedy.[47] She was *entering into* their beliefs, but neither pretending she had theirs, nor obtruding her own.

2.13. LEGITIMATE QUESTIONING OF RELIGIONS

Despite recommending voluntary boundaries to religious disputes, I should insist that there can be legitimate criticism, reform, and questioning of religion. Mill's requirement of understanding the opposing case does not mean that one must leave adherents of that case to do what they like. Gandhi criticized the practices of his fellow co-religionists towards the group then called Untouchables, and now called the Dalits, or the oppressed, when he compared the treatment of them by his fellow Hindus with the conduct of the most hated of British officers in India from 1919.[48] In England, we would not want Chaucer to have been prevented from parodying in his *Pardoner's Tale* the extortionate practitioners of religious agents who took money in return for their purported ability

47. Richard Sorabji, *The Untold Story of Cornelia Sorabji, Reformer, Lawyer and Champion of Women's Rights in India*, I. B. Tauris, London, and Penguin India, New Delhi, 2010.
48. 'The spinning-wheel movement', *Navajivan*, 26 February 1921; speech at suppressed classes conference, *Young India*, 27 April and 4 May 1921, electronic *Collected Works* (eCW) vol. 22, p. 316 and vol. 23, p. 44.

to redeem sins and guarantee eternal salvation of souls. Many Western countries allow quite savage satire against their own political rulers. Within their own community, that can be a good tradition, as a counterbalance against the temptations of power. Where the political rulers are religious rulers, the temptations of power are at least as great.

In these examples, people were speaking to members of groups with which they identified. But one may also criticize the social practices or the religious head of groups *other* than one's own, except that criticism is less likely to be persuasive, and will sometimes even be counterproductive. That is especially so, if one criticizes the revered ancient founder of a religion, both because it is unlikely to be persuasive, and because it tarnishes all members of that religion, whatever their practices. Moreover, it is not the ancient founder, but only the current interpretations and uses of the founder, that one has any hope of modifying. A contrary decision was made in a lawsuit in British India, that a scurrilous attack, condemned by Gandhi, on the founder of the Muslim religion had not been shown to be meant as an attack on the Muslim religion as such. This implausible decision was one of the disturbing factors that led to an amendment of the Indian Penal Code to include the new section 295A, making it a crime to outrage religious feelings with deliberate and malicious intention.[49] However, the *current* leaders of a religion are in a different position if exercising *political* power as

49. Abhinav Chandrachud, *Republic of Rhetoric, Free Speech and the Constitution of India*, Penguin Viking, Gurgaon, 2017, pp. 228–230.

religious leaders. Then safeguards are required as much as for *non*-religious political leaders, although different sensitivities will be called for. There have been cases in which members of different religions happily shared in each other's lives, until religious *politicians* insisted on religious divisions.[50]

There is also the possibility of legal reform of practices provided that they are within one's jurisdiction. In the debates of 1946–1949 in the Indian Constituent Assembly about establishing the Indian Constitution, the idea grew that equal rights should belong to all Indian citizens regardless of their religion. Accordingly, Article 25.2 of the Indian Constitution saw it as permissible to impose social reform by introducing laws *restricting* certain economic, financial, or political constraints associated with religious practice, for example concerning the rights of women, or providing for *social welfare or reform* in religions. Consequently, the Hindu Code Bills of 1956 interfered with some social practices in Hinduism. In 1986, the law intervened also in a certain Muslim practice, in the case of Shah Bano, after her Muslim husband said that Muslim domestic law allowed him to pay his wife, on divorcing her, only three months of financial maintenance. The courts cited the criminal code to strike this down, although politicians restored the practice.[51] In the United Kingdom, British law is available to

---

50. Such an interpretation of one-time *local* religious politicians in Baluchistan is provided by Reena Nanda, in *From Quetta to Delhi*, Bloomsbury, London, 2018. The British implementation of the religious divisions has been widely criticized still more, though as political, not as religious.
51. Rochana Bajpai, *Debating Difference: Group Rights and Liberal Democracy in India*, Oxford University Press, New Delhi, 2011.

British Muslims, who can appeal to the law against any practice in their own religion which is forbidden under British law.

Different from criticism of religious practices, but at least as legitimate, is the seeker's questioning. To take an ancient Greek example, Porphyry (232/3–309 CE) was not only a philosopher with his own views, but also a scholar of the history of ideas and a questioner of views in many spheres. Though religious himself, he was a seeker of truth, and in that spirit questioned the religion of his fellow Greeks and fellow Platonists, some of whom favoured Egyptian religion, as well as questioning Jewish and Christian religion. He thought that the highest god required only the sacrifice of purifying one's mind, and so opposed animal sacrifice at least for philosophers, even if the minds of other people could not hope to connect with that god.[52] Writing to his younger colleague, the priestly Iamblichus, who favoured Egyptian religion, Porphyry probed the practices, not disrespectfully but searchingly, asking for explanations of how his priestly rituals could work. They surely could not lead us back to God, but at best help to purify emotions.[53] But then why did Iamblichus favour including erotic festivals in religious worship?[54] Iamblichus's reply was haughty, but ingenious: he cited Aristotle's belief in catharsis,

52. Pure mind: Porphyry, *On Abstinence from Killing Animals*, 2.61. Others may not be able to take that route, 1.27; 3.2.
53. Porphyry, *On the Return of the Soul*, reported in Augustine, *City of God*, 10.9.
54. Porphyry's questions from his *Letter to Anebo* are included with Iamblichus's answers in Iamblichus, *On the Mysteries of the Egyptians*, translated by E. C. Clarke, John Dillon, and J. P. Hershbell, Brill, Leiden, 2003.

taken as the purging of emotion, now including erotic emotion, through moderate arousal.

In his *Return of the Soul*,[55] Porphyry says in another exchange that in all his searches he has not found a universal road to liberation of the soul, not among the truest of philosophies (Platonism), or the Indians, or the Chaldaeans. The Christian Augustine, rightly or wrongly, took him to mean a road that is for everyone both a necessary and a sufficient route. It was a major theme of Porphyry, as in chapter 1 we found it later to be of Themistius and his pupil Julian, that there are many roads to God and to happiness. He says to Iamblichus in his *Letter to Anebo*, 'The road to happiness can surely be different'.[56] Again, the Church historian Eusebius records Porphyry citing in his *Philosophy from Oracles* the oracle of Apollo as saying that there are many paths (*pollai atrapoi*) or roads leading to the gods. Porphyry emphasizes the relevance to religious tolerance when he says that the roads were revealed first to non-Greeks, the Egyptians, and then to Phoenicians, Chaldaeans, Lydians, and Hebrews.[57] The dispassionate, inquiring tone of his *Letter to Anebo* makes me doubt that he can have been the rabid enemy of Christians that many Christians believed him to be. Among his writings which they (not he) called 'Against the Christians', was one in which, writing as a scholar, he argued that the Judaeo-Christian Book of Daniel cannot have

55. Reported Augustine, *City of God*, 10.32.
56. Iamblichus, *On the Mysteries of the Egyptians*, 10.1.
57. Eusebius, *Praeparatio Evangelica*, 9. 10.1–5 = fragments 323 F, 324 F, in A. Smith, *Porphyrii philosophi fragmenta*, Teubner 1993.

been a book of prophecy, because it was written *after* the events described, a conclusion which modern Christian scholarship has confirmed. Nonetheless, the Christian Augustine repeatedly shows respect, and calls him the most learned (*doctissimus*) of the philosophers, though the sharpest (*acerrimus*) enemy of the Christians.[58] 'Learned' and 'sharp' surely account for Augustine's paying him so much attention. But another Christian, Eusebius, reacted, in parallel with Iamblichus's haughtiness, with strong hostility.

2.14. SUMMARY OF CONCLUSION

I have discussed many cases in which the law has been used, or might usefully be used, to provide boundaries on freedom of speech. But legislation is always difficult, and instead I have looked for a boundary that we protagonists of free speech should accept voluntarily as derived from the benefits of free speech. My two main proposals, in this context, based on consideration of various different cultures and times, have been, first, that a new important boundary for free speech would be the line at which it frustrates its own good purposes. Secondly, when insistence on free speech as a right frustrates discussion, there have been many forms of persuasive speech that can still

---

58. Augustine, *City of God*, 19.22, emphasized by Gillian Clark, 'Augustine's Porphyry and the universal way of salvation', in George Karamanolis and Anne Sheppard, eds., *Studies on Porphyry*, Bulletin of the Institute of Classical Studies, supplement 98, pp. 127–140, at p. 130.

open ears, when insistence on free speech cannot. There may still be a call, in some cases, for frank speech, but knowing what speech to use to open ears is an art. This is important at times of national disagreement, as, for example, the divisive politics in the United Kingdom which led in 2019 to Britain leaving the European Union (Brexit).

The UK Parliament at one time was good at using wit to forestall conflict. My aunt, Cornelia Sorabji, in a letter home to India, described watching, as guest of the Speaker Arthur Wellesley Peel, a debate in Parliament on 1 February 1893, on an earlier thorny question: Home Rule for Ireland. Colonel Sanderson called Father MacFadyn a ruffian—howls of protest—and indeed a murderous ruffian. Prime Minister William Gladstone, advocate of the Second Home Rule Bill for Ireland, rose and spoke about patience. The Speaker then ruled and Colonel Sanderson responded, 'I yield. I withdraw 'murderous ruffian' and substitute 'excited politician'.[59]

---

59. Cornelia Sorabji, European manuscripts F165/6, The British Library, 1 February 1893, with further reference 4 February.

Chapter 3

Free speech on social media

*How to protect our freedoms from those
social media that are funded by trade in our
personal data*

I have so far recommended personal awareness of the benefits of
free speech and voluntary self-restraint in using speech which damages those benefits. But sometimes there is no alternative to legal
control. This, I believe, is the case with a major present-day problem: the maximisation of profit by some social media companies
by revenue from advertising, including propaganda. The advertising is not necessarily regulated, since anyone may advertise. It can
be enhanced through the use of personal profiles constructed by
inference from the personal data entered by users and from elsewhere. Personal profiles can be used, for example, to target different users of social media with differently worded advertisements,
including propaganda, designed to influence different profiles.

Freedom of Speech and Expression. Richard Sorabji, Oxford University Press (2021). © Oxford
University Press. DOI: 10.1093/oso/9780197532157.003.0003

Controls are needed that are more effective than the fines, which at present have little effect on sufficiently profitable companies. But first the rather tiresome attempt must be made to follow reports on how the funding systems are said to work.

The online tech companies have brought us great benefits in almost instantaneous access both to information and to communication. The first of the very big tech companies, though not the first altogether, was Google, founded in the United States in 1998.[1] It provided a very useful service in allowing users to search online for information far more extensive than any printed encyclopaedia could offer, and with the advantage of being constantly updated, and this is not going to be lost. Facebook, founded in the United States in 2006, expanded in the direction of online conversations across national boundaries between indefinitely many people, independently of the use of email. These were great and pioneering advantages. But I shall pick out some of the problems that seem to have accompanied the funding methods used. These methods are sometimes rather secretive, so I depend on studies published by authors and by governmental inquiries, which I shall cite. I make no claim to more direct knowledge of how any social media operate. Moreover, methods of operation change all the time, so that readers would need to check how they have changed. But I think that the problems will not be dealt with if most of the public does not know about some of the methods

---

1. I take the following information on Google from Soshana Zuboff, *The Age of Surveillance Capitalism*, Profile Books, London, 2019, pp. 71–86, 93, 113, 117, 511.

used up to the present, so that a short account could be useful, even if second-hand.

Although I shall mention Facebook most often among the social media, this is chiefly because its pioneering techniques have been the most discussed in the literature. Many other social media use some of the same techniques, which indeed started well before the creation of Facebook. I will describe first how the company grew out of the founder's student experiments.

3.1. THE CREATION OF FACEBOOK

Facebook was launched worldwide with a useful mission in 2006 by Mark Zuckerberg. He had created the first of his clever inventions as a Harvard student in 2003 with a new, if rather insouciant, type of website. He is said[2] to have hacked the identification photos of fellow students and placed two next to each other at a time, asking users to vote for the more attractive person. He then wrote codes to compute rankings and ranked the identified Harvard students according to attractiveness. He received 22,000 votes in one day, or, on another account, in four hours. Harvard made him take the site down, and he went on to create instead a Harvard version of a student directory or 'facebook' with identifying

2. Katharine A. Kaplan, *The Harvard Crimson*, 19 November 2003.

photos online, which then spread to other universities. Subsequently, in 2006, he launched its successor worldwide with new features as the Facebook we know. It still used photos, but also offered users an online space for chatting with 'friends', and without needing to have an email account, but allowing instead for chatting across national boundaries and with indefinitely large numbers of people. The chatting, as on email, was not face to face, nor as on the telephone with audible tones of voice, but in writing. However, in 2012 Mark Zuckerberg was to buy the company Instagram for exchanging the photos. The chatting was intended to prove addictive, and Facebook succeeded in bringing an incomparable number of people together to exchange data on the platform. There were, as of June 2018, 2.2 billion users,[3] more than a billion of them using the site every day. Sometimes the chatting is autobiographical, but equally when it is about other things, it reveals differences of opinion and character and users can create followers, whom they are encouraged to count.

There is no doubt that Mark Zuckerberg is a very clever man, that his inventions have created huge changes, and that the overall benefit could be great if the problems were addressed. I believe they could be addressed and that they stem largely from the optional choice of funding methodology.

---

3. Jacob Weisberg, 'The autocracy app', *New York Review of Books* 65.16, 25 October–7 November 2018, p. 22.

3.2. THE USE OF PERSONAL PROFILES DERIVED FROM OUR FOOTPRINTS ON SOCIAL MEDIA FOR TARGETING INDIVIDUALS WITH ADVERTISEMENTS, INCLUDING POLITICAL PROPAGANDA

One problem described in the literature is that it has proved possible for some social media companies to make record-breaking profits by a particular method of funding: the highly lucrative use of personal profiles on behalf of paying advertisers, or the free exchange of personal profiles or other personal data between social media companies. Commercial advertisers confine their interest to data or profiles only about your interests, so that they can conjecture what you might want to buy. But advertisements can come also from propagandists of varied kinds, who want to persuade you to support things quite different from sales income. They may work on behalf of undisclosed interests. The aims of some may not be desirable, and they may use disinformation to persuade. For persuasion, they might find profiles of your character and susceptibilities more useful than profiles of your interests. Through personal profiles based on data from users' footprints, Facebook and some other social media companies seek to target users with messages diversified to attract their particular profile, rather than with messages that have been verified. We shall see in the following that personal profiles can be used for swinging elections. It can be particularly difficult to verify the messages of politicians, and this could well be why Facebook has felt obliged to restrict its recent reform of banning false claims in advertising by exempting from verification any website or webpage which has the 'primary purpose of expressing the opinion or agenda of a political figure'.[4]

According to a report of 11 July 2019 by the United Kingdom's Information Commissioner's Office, *Democracy Disrupted?* (p. 39), Facebook claimed that it assessed interests, not characteristics. But according to p. 38 of the report, Facebook, like Twitter, Google, and Snapchat (p. 41), did not make clear that advertising included *political* advertising. So the reader is left unclear whether political advertising did or did not assess character or susceptibilities as well as interests. Page 40, note 19, of the report states that homosexual interest was targeted with advertisements by Facebook, according to a study by Madrid University. This illustrates that even commercial profiling of interests can be intrusive.

The founder of Facebook, Mark Zuckerberg, prefers to speak of trading rather than selling for some purposes. In an oral testimony to Senator Cornyn, he described the advertising process as 'showing the ads to the right people without that data changing hands and going to the advertiser'. I think this may mean that users' personal data, and possibly the resulting profiles, are not sold to advertisers, along with advertising space, but are only used to create and send to customers

---

4. *The Guardian*, Alex Hern, 5 October 2019.

the advertisement for which the advertiser pays. But Michael Kosinski has objected that, although Facebook does the targeting, it can be the advertiser who creates the initial profile of the class of people it wants to reach, in which case something *is* sold to the advertiser: knowledge of which individuals fit that profile. As he puts it, 'If a ski shop pays Facebook to show an ad only to women, then Facebook automatically reveals to the ski shop that all people who clicked on the link [in response to the advertisement] must be women. And in practice, the advertisers make requests that are much more nuanced. They may ask Facebook to show their ad to "liberal Latina women without college education who live in San Antonio and recently got married". And then they might place a separate ad that is shown only to "conservative African-American women with college educations who live in Austin and are single". When you click on an ad and are sent to an advertiser's website, the advertiser knows which ad you saw and thus which bucket you fall in'.[5]

Facebook offers help to advertisers not only by profiling *existing* clients, but also towards finding *new* clients by using the profiles of 'look-alike' groups of people, who seem to have similar traits to existing clients and might therefore be easy to interest.[6] Facebook does not define precisely how it measures

5. Michael Kosinski in the *New York Times*, 12 December 2018, in his 'Congress may have fallen for Facebook's trap, but you don't have to'.
6. Martin Moore, *Democracy Hacked*, One World Books, London, 2018, p. 121.

similarity, nor does it disclose its algorithms for selecting the look-alike groups.[7]

Personal profiles may be compiled from various different data. Since social media exchange personal data with each other and with other companies, one company might be able to pool its data about what people have searched, another about what they have contemplated buying, and another about what they have said online. In the United Kingdom, the exchange of personal data between companies was described in the Final Report of the House of Commons Digital, Culture, Media and Sport Committee of February 2019, entitled *Disinformation and 'fake news'*.[8] It quoted emails from within the Facebook company, three of them about maximizing revenue by exchanging data, and written by the founder Mark Zuckerberg himself[9] in October and November 2012. The emails were working out a policy of raising revenue by sharing personal profiles of Facebook users with certain companies in return for receiving data from their users, thus increasing the value of the Facebook network.[10] Facebook allowed (paragraph 84) access to profiles to 5,200 'apps', including Netflix, AirBnB, and the

---

7. Athanasios Andreou, Marcio Silva, Fabricio Benevenuto, Oana Goga, Patrick Loiseau, and others, 'Measuring the Facebook advertising ecosystem', HAL, submitted 18 December 2018, https://hal.archives-ouvertes.fr/hal-01959145
8. *Disinformation and 'fake news', Final Report of the House of Commons Digital, Culture, Media and Sport Committee*, 2019, paragraphs 64–76.
9. Ibid., paragraphs 97, 98, and 105.
10. Even more of the emails had been cited in the committee's Interim Report in July 2018, and a number of these emails were summarized in *The Guardian*, by Alex Hern, 6 December 2018.

taxi app Lyft, and the price for access in Autumn 2013 (paragraph 100) was US$250,000 a year, or 'equivalent contributions'.[11] In addition, access to Facebook users' profiles was allowed (paragraph 27), in return for exchange of information, to such major internet companies as Microsoft, Amazon, and Spotify. On the other hand, apps or networks that were seen as unwanted competitors, such as that of the company Six4Three, claimed to have been frozen out from access to personal profiles, so that they went bankrupt. It was from the court case brought against Facebook by Six4Three that the same House of Commons committee in the United Kingdom obtained some of the documents outlining Facebook's strategy. The Final UK Report of 2019 also spoke of earlier confrontations between the Federal Trade commission in the United States and Facebook about the exchange of personal profiles in return for equivalent contributions.[12]

It will emerge later in connection with propaganda for swinging elections that another technique was used with Facebook's knowledge by Christopher Wylie of Cambridge Analytica, who confessed to using an internet application that could not only harvest the personal data of Facebook users, but also enhance it many times over by harvesting the data of

11. Such as access to the data of the app *users*, or permission to use the app company's trademark names.
12. In 2011, the Commission was said to have complained that Facebook had been violating privacy since 2007 by sharing profiles on this basis. The Commission offered to make a settlement with Facebook. But in 2012, it complained that, despite the settlement, a Facebook user's profile could also be accessed by platform applications that were used by the user's 'friends'.

Facebook 'friends' of any user, to create personality profiles of that user. Facebook thus knew that somebody was creating personality profiles from their data, and asked him only for assurance that it was for academic purposes. Their subsequent objection to him was that they did not know that he was selling the profiles commercially.

Personal profiles can also be compiled from other sources. One source, used by diverse parties, is the tracking devices called web bugs, which had been installed long before Facebook, even in the 1990s, in websites and emails in order to track user activity.[13] Web bugs can collect our personal data if we insouciantly click on them and can then return advertising messages to us. Facebook also collects data and profiles from unregulated data-broking companies.[14] Data brokers are companies that buy up data, not always accurate, from a large range of sources and sell it to people who want information about you.[15] The personal profiles based on these mixed sources can be supplemented by *inferences* from the personal data so gained.

13. See e.g. Zuboff, *The Age of Surveillance Capitalism*, p. 86.
14. Tim Sparapani interview on *The Facebook Dilemma*; discussed also by Sue Halpern, 'Apologize later', *New York Review of Books* 66.1, 17 January–6 February 2019, reviewing *The Facebook Dilemma*. The data brokers are unregulated, despite a full Federal Trade Commission report.
15. See Information Commissioner's Office, *Investigation into the Use of Data Analytics in Political Campaigns*, 11 July 2018, 4.6, and 'What are 'Data Brokers' and why are they scooping up information about you?' https://motherboard.vice.com/en_us/article/bjpx3w/what-are-data-brokers-and-how-to-stop-my-private-data-collection.

3.3. JEOPARDIZING THE DEMOCRATIC VOTE

One problem about trading in profiles with advertisers is that the advertisers are not only the commercial advertisers whom the name might suggest. They can include propagandists who want to swing elections without voters knowing what has happened. The information contained in personal profiles is unprecedently rich, and propagandists can use differentiated disinformation targeted to different voters to play on individual susceptibilities ascertained from the profiles. The facilitation of targeted propaganda has been carried out not only by Facebook but by a number of social media companies, and later I shall mention Twitter, also founded in 2006.

Another result of targeting different content to different recipients on the basis of different profiles is that people are kept in separate echo chambers, as they have been called, hearing what echoes their own opinions, rather than learning the truth. Truth is a casualty, and this matters particularly when the content is political.

When personal profiles based on free speech are used to target *voters*, the practice can make a mockery of the democratic vote. One reason why the practice is so damaging is that democracy depends on the readiness of voters who lose to accept that more of their fellow citizens have freely chosen to vote the other way. If their fellow citizens' vote has not been free, but manipulated, where is the basis for accepting the result? What has happened in this case is that profiles based on our free speech have been used to nullify a particularly important act of free speech, one's vote. It is significant that one's vote is called one's 'voice' in Russian.

3.4. BETTER METHODOLOGIES
FOR FUNDING SOCIAL MEDIA

There are other social media that do not seek record-breaking profits by trading in personal profiles. They need to be encouraged. Many of them may use an earlier and better method of funding social media by *subscription* from users. And this would be better still if subscriptions were varied according to ability to pay in different countries or parts of a country. But there are other acceptable methods of funding too. DuckDuckGo does not use your personal data, when you search for information. It allows advertisers to promote items connected not with your personal data, but with the search term you used. And if your search results in a sale from Amazon or eBay, it also gains a commission from those sellers.

But these more acceptable methods of funding have regrettably been bypassed by those media which make their huge profits instead by trading in personal profiles. As a result, I think that many users do not know why the latter services are free of charge to them. It is important that the public should know the method used. The case for funding by subscription has been impressively made by others. In 2010 John Lanchester pointed, as one alternative model, to the subscription system of Spotify, which is able to charge subscriptions for online music, because the range of music offered was so enormous,[16] as is true also of the range of posts and advertisements on Facebook. Tim Berners-Lee, the founder of the World Wide Web, was still suggesting in 2017[17] that social media on the internet might avoid depending on advertisers for their costs, if they depended instead on subscriptions and micropayments from users. I shall come later to some evidence that younger users are tired of seeing so many political advertisements, which might suggest that they would welcome a return to a different funding method.

An admirable alternative method of funding recently on the rise is *donation* from users,[18] but it depends on a high level of *trust* on the part of users. *The Guardian* newspaper, at the time of creating its *online* edition, started requesting

---

16. John Lanchester, 'Let us pay', *London Review of Books*, December 2010. I am grateful to Professor Maja Korica of Warwick University, who first drew my attention in September 2017 to John Lanchester's article and to many others of 2016–2017. I set aside here controversies about whether musicians have been properly reimbursed.

17. Tim Berners Lee, Sunday, 12 March 2017, available at https://www.theguardian.com/technology/2017/mar/11/tim-berners-lee-web-inventor-save-internet

18. Nic Newman, *Reuters Institute for the Study of Journalism Digital News Report 2018, Overview and Key Findings*, pp. 36–37, 41–44, http://www.digitalnewsreport.org/survey/2018/overview-key-findings-2018/, and Newman, *Reuters Institute for the Study of Journalism Digital News Report 2018*, 2.5, 'Donations and crowdfunding: An emerging opportunity?'.

donations in 2016 and had soon raised 600,000 voluntary payments, raising tens of millions of UK pounds each year. It also crowdfunded its 2018 reporting of school shootings in the United States. Although most donations came from online readers in the United States, and only 1% donate to news organizations in the United Kingdom, 22% of a UK sample said they might be willing to donate to a news organization in the future, if they felt it could not cover costs in other ways. In other polls across different countries, almost one in five of those not already paying said that they were likely to do so in the next twelve months. Voluntary donation has a social advantage over graded subscription, in that the voluntariness of the donation avoids a system in which quality news reaches only those who can afford it.

When in 2014 Facebook bought up the company WhatsApp, the latter company at that time respected the privacy of users' data, by funding itself not through selling personal data to advertisers, but through a very modest user *subscription* of 99 US cents per year—less than one US dollar. Facebook, however is reported to have bought up WhatsApp to gain the lucrative personal data on its users, without initially charging for its use at all, and to have pooled the data of the two companies.[19] The data explicitly mentioned here were data on the *behaviour* of users. In May 2017, the European Union fined Facebook

---

19. Zuboff, *The Age of Surveillance Capitalism*, p. 103, with note 20.

US$122 million for 'misleading' statements about the takeover of WhatsApp.[20] Facebook's founder Mark Zuckerberg is also alleged[21] to have assured the founders of WhatsApp that he would not share their users' data with other applications, and to have told the European Union, which approved the merger, that he had no way of matching the two sets of users. But it is reported[22] that when Facebook found a way, it connected the two sets of users and sold to advertisers the profiles of WhatsApp users. Other private search engines which to different degrees protect our searches from being tracked, besides DuckDuck Go, include Start page and Search Encrypt.

It is a mistaken idea that the collection of personal data is something good in itself.[23] But on the other hand, not all collection of personal data is illegitimate. I myself would have been interested to know whether the books in a series I started were catering, as intended, for non-specialists as well as specialists, and it could have helped me to cater better for non-specialists if I had known who was buying the books. I have no personal objection to Amazon recording the history of books I have bought online from them, in order to tell me of other books I might like, so long as they are not selling the data to others.

20. *The Guardian*, Jennifer Rankin, 18 May 2017.
21. Weisberg, 'The autocracy app', p. 22.
22. Ibid., p. 20.
23. Compare the view that data processing is always a worthy good, criticized in Woodrow Hartzog and Neil Richards, 'Privacy's constitutional moment and the limits of data protection', *Boston College Law Review* 2020 (79 pages in pre-print), p. 1. https://papers.ssrn.com/sol3/papers.cfm?abstract_id=3441502

3.5. HOW MUCH IS REVEALED TO USERS ABOUT THE CONSTRUCTION OF THEIR PROFILES?

It already seems somewhat surprising that Facebook did not ask its users if it might trade in their personal data. Of course, many users might have agreed to the trading, at least before they knew how their personal data would be re-used, because they were getting a very great benefit, free access to conversation across the world on the new social media. But as they were not asked, many would have been aware only of the benefit. I believe that only a minority of users know what makes it possible for their use of social media to be free of charge to them. I think the others would be well advised to read Facebook's own Data Policy[24], which succinctly answers such questions as, 'What kinds of information do we collect?' and 'How do we use this information?' To some readers it may seem like an astonishing confession what kind of private information is collected and how it is used. Other readers will not be surprised at all, but many may well begin to feel anxious. Given the slow development of privacy law in general in the United Kingdom and the United States, as described in the appendix to this chapter, it may be less surprising that, even with recent reforms, social media have not yet progressed very far with the protection of privacy.

24. Data Policy, https://www.facebook.com/about/privacy/your-info

Facebook users are allowed to see what has been retained from the personal data entered by themselves, but until recently not any *inferences* made from the data to create a profile of them.[25] Nor are users allowed to see the *algorithms* used to select the different messages to be shown to different profiles.[26] However, recently, in response to complaints about privacy violation, Facebook has introduced two privacy mechanisms, as described in at least two papers of 2018.[27] One mechanism is a button asking with reference to an advertisement received by a user, 'Why am I seeing this?' Another is an attribute, or list of attributes, *inferred* by Facebook to belong to a given user, with some explanation of the inference. The median number of attributes inferred by Facebook in the tests run by one study was 310. But both of Facebook's innovations have been judged by the articles in question to be of distinctly limited value. It is said that Facebook has provided to advertisers a choice of 200,000 attributes they might want to target in their advertisements, and that advertisers have been known to choose up to

---

25. Final Report of the House of Commons Digital, Culture, Media and Sport Committee, 18 February 2019, paragraphs 41–42; Zuboff, *The Age of Surveillance Capitalism*, pp. 483–484.
26. Final Report, Digital (etc.), paragraphs 19, 49, 150, 315; Zuboff, *The Age of Surveillance Capitalism*, pp. 186–187, 484–485.
27. I draw here again on Athanasios Andreou and others, 'Measuring the Facebook advertising ecosystem', and on Athanasios Andreou, Giridhari Ventkatadri, Oana Goga, Krishna P. Gummadi, Patrick Loiseau, and Alan Mislove, 'Investigating ad transparency mechanisms in social media: A case study of Facebook's explanations', Network and Distributed Systems Security, Symposium 18–21 February 2018, San Diego, California, http://dx.doi.org/10.14722/ndss.2018.23191

105 attributes at a time for targeting.[28] But despite these numbers, as regards the 'Why am I seeing this?' button, Facebook does not list more than one attribute to explain why a given advertisement is being seen. The attribute chosen tends to be one widespread among users, so that more intrusive attributes, such as family and relationships, including 'open relationships', are not so likely to be revealed.[29] Facebook does, on the other hand, provide an 'Ad preference page' on which it lists all the attributes it has inferred about a user. These include especially the user's *interests*, which may have been inferred from the user's expression of 'likes', interest shown by the user's investigating particular advertisements or advertiser web pages, or by downloading of particular 'apps' (applications). Also listed is behavioural and demographic information about the user. It is not, however, specified what page was 'liked' or what advertisement investigated. So the explanation of attributes inferred is rather vague.[30]

Besides targeting certain attributes, advertisers since 2012 have been allowed to target individuals uniquely identified by their email addresses, phone numbers, names, and zip (or postal) codes.[31] But it is not revealed to the user which of these identifying features has been used.[32]

---

28. Andreou and others, 'Measuring the Facebook advertising ecosystem'; 'Investigating ad transparency mechanisms in social media', p. 11.

29. Ibid., pp. 9, 10.

30. Ibid., p. 12.

31. Ibid., pp. 3 and 5.

32. Ibid., p. 11.

When Facebook draws personal data from data brokers, using in the United States the four firms Epsilon, DLX, Experian, and Acxiom, it does not specify any inferred attributes.[33]

One extra transparency, however, is that in the 'newsfeed' which Facebook feeds to its different users, it does distinguish advertisements by marking them as 'sponsored'.[34]

I believe that at least with profiles such as can be used for political purposes, the law should require users to be allowed to see the inferences made about them and the various resulting profiles, and it should be made clear to all users that such data and inferences are being used to make profiles of them and for what purposes.

I also believe it should be made easy for suitable national watchdogs, such as the UK's Information Commissioner's Office and Electoral Commission, to see who are purchasing advertisements for targeting personal profiles for political purposes, and the advertisements or propaganda should carry information on who is sponsoring them.

On 2 August 2019, Jim Waterson in *The Guardian*[35] alleged that this was evaded in propaganda presented on Facebook by Lynton Crosby's Australian lobbying firm, CTF Partners.

---

33. Ibid., p. 11.
34. Andreou and others, 'Measuring the Facebook advertising ecosystem', p. 3.
35. This goes far beyond an earlier report in *The Guardian* by Jim Waterson, 4–5 April, 2019, on CTF Partners' propaganda.

According to some of their past and present employees, along with internal documents, the firm was alleged to work initially by creating a Facebook page purporting to be an independent news source, but containing what was called disinformation on behalf of its paying customers. The customers were said to include coal and tobacco companies, opponents of cyclists, political advocates of an extreme form of British exit ('Brexit') from the European Union, and one side in a war with a strategy of killing civilians. According to this account, the Facebook page was given names such as 'Middle East Diplomat' to suggest impartiality, or 'Make Greens Honest' to query their reception of subsidies for ecological practice. It could then present what looked like a grassroots movement of support, which had in fact been coordinated by employees of CTF partners. Facebook was further alleged to waive its protection against 'coordinated inauthentic behaviour', if the coordination was made under the name of one person who could be called a 'business manager'. Some messages of support reportedly came in from personal email accounts, others from encrypted email accounts to avoid being traced, some bearing only initials, not names. The names of some CTF writers were reported to be known to Facebook, but not passed to the public. According to Waterson's report, the resulting propaganda was then targeted at millions of people, using Facebook's targeting tools, including the personal profiles of supporters and Facebook's look-alike groups, mentioned earlier.

3.6. THE NEED TO SELL ADVERTISING SPACE WITHIN SENSATIONAL OR EXTREMIST WEBPAGES PRIORITIZES EXTREMIST POLITICIANS, GLAMORIZES VIOLENCE

A different kind of problem, also serious, comes from social media selling advertising space to advertisers and placing their advertisements within sensational or extremist content, which is more widely read, so that the media can charge advertisers more. Sensational content can be supplied on extremist websites hosted by the media. One example supplied by *Private Eye*[36] concerned advertisements placed by Google, not Facebook, on extremist websites which in some cases supported causes opposite to those of the companies who were advertising. The extremist sites were allowed by Google to gain income when readers visited the advertisements they hosted.

Sensation can be produced by messages of hate, intimidation, indecency, descriptions of self-harm and suicide, some of which have further suicidal consequences, or by depictions of scenes of terrorist murders which incite further terrorism. Sensational information may be collected from sources that are themselves putting out false information. One effect that has been noticed in political news on social media during election campaigns is that candidates who looked to the middle

---

36. *Private Eye*, 18 October 2019.

ground and sought consensus gained fewer followers than polarizing candidates who were emotionally exciting. If so, the social media, even if unintentionally, have favoured extremist election results.[37] Another effect is glamorizing violence and self-harm.

The *Private Eye* report announced some recent success for a counter-movement, the Stop Funding Fake News Campaign. It informed the advertisers, which included the UK Parliament, of the websites on which their advertisements had been placed, and many withdrew their advertisements, thereby reducing the profitability of the scheme.

3.7. WHY IT IS DIFFICULT FOR SOCIAL MEDIA TO REMOVE GENOCIDAL CONTENT, APPEALS TO BURN MEMBERS OF RACIAL GROUPS, SCENES OF MASS MURDER, AND OTHER EXTREMISM

There are genuine difficulties for social media in removing content when it becomes too extremist, even when it tries. This makes the methodology dangerous even when that is not intended. The United Nations accused social media, and Facebook in particular, of playing a significant role in the genocide of the Rohingya people in Myanmar, by hosting without

37. Moore, *Democracy Hacked*, p. 114.

correction the propaganda against those people which facilitated the subsequent genocide.[38] Particularly horrifying was the live streaming on Facebook on 15 March 2019, shared by Twitter and Google's YouTube, of fifty victims, including children, being killed in a New Zealand mosque by a gun-wielding hater of Muslims, who deliberately streamed his own action to the media. What were the problems in taking such content down?

It is often hard to have enough editors of content. When Facebook hosted the propaganda that the United Nations cited as playing a significant role in subsequent genocide against the Rohingya people, it had at first no staff in Myanmar who spoke the language to serve as editors of the propaganda, although it later brought some in. That, at any rate, was reported by the US public broadcast service TV programme *Frontline*'s *The Facebook Dilemma*, of 25–26 October 2018. It is in any case hard to have enough editors of content skilled in the languages of different countries, and in Nigeria in 2019 Facebook was said to have only four.[39]

The use of web robots, instead of people, to remove undesirable content may sometimes seem sensible, because robots can pick out certain undesirable words faster than humans. However, in order to correct a recent campaign by Jew-haters who were asking how to burn Jews, Facebook is said to have

---

38. As stated in an interview by Kara Swisher of Facebook's founder, Mark Zuckerberg, on the US public broadcast service TV programme *Frontline*'s *The Facebook Dilemma*, of 25–26 October 2018.
39. Halpern, 'Apologise later', reviewing *The Facebook Dilemma*.

brought in more human editors instead.[40] But how are enough humans to be employed? In Germany,[41] to avoid new German fines of up to 50 million euros (originally £44 million), 500 employees of internet platforms have been enlisted to edit platform content. But can this practice be followed in all countries?

Another problem is that editing out content involves moral understanding and does not lend itself to reliable *general rules* which can be taught to humans or programmed into web robots. An illustration of the difficulty was Facebook's temporary removal of the famous image of a naked nine-year-old girl running away in the Vietnam War, her back burnt by napalm, an important illustration of the horror of the Vietnam War. There was nothing sexually indecent about the image, but it was wrongly so treated and removed on that ground.[42]

Frontline's The Facebook Dilemma, of 25–26 October 2018 recorded another problem, the experience of Max Schrems when he asked the European Data Protection Commission in Ireland to remove his personal data. What he found was that the data were stored in so many places that they were automatically retrieved, and reloaded after initial deletion.[43] This reloading of

40. Zeynep Tufekci, 'Facebook's "Ad" scandal isn't a "fail", it's a feature', *New York Times*, 23 September 2017; Julia Angwin, Madeleine Varner, and Ariana Tobin, 'Facebook enabled advertisers to reach "Jew haters"', *ProPublica*, September 14, 2017, https://www.propublica.org/article/facebook-enabled-advertisers-to-reach-jew-haters

41. BBC News, 1 January, 2018, https://www.bbc.co.uk/news/technology-42510868

42. Sam Thielman, *The Guardian*, 26 August 2016; Sam Levin, Julia Carrie Wong, Luke Harding, 'Facebook backs down from "napalm girl" censorship and reinstates photo', *The Guardian*, 9 September 2016.

43. Frontline's *The Facebook Dilemma*, of 25–26 October 2018.

data also affected the very slow removal by Facebook, Twitter, and Google's YouTube of the terrorist's video of fifty people being killed by his gunfire in a New Zealand mosque on Friday, 15 March 2019. After 24 hours, Facebook, whatever the figures for Twitter and YouTube, had removed only 1.5 million accounts that were showing the video,[44] even though the display was an encouragement to like-minded terrorists. This does not sound as if the social media are in control of editing requirements.

3.8. EFFECT ON PUBLIC LIFE AND ON MENTAL AND PHYSICAL HEALTH OF A CLIMATE OF PERSONAL ABUSE ONLINE AND OFFLINE

The ease with which personal abuse can be delivered online may have increased personal abuse offline as well. This was illustrated when, upon the announcement of a UK general election in November 2019, many Members of Parliament, especially women, declined to stand for election again, citing personal abuse online and offline. But I should now add to this the effects on mental and physical health, which have been well described by others. Jean Twenge, in her book *i-Gen*,[45] has described the anxiety induced in teenagers of the internet

44. *The Washington Post*, 17 March 2019.
45. Jean Twenge, *I-Gen*, Simon and Schuster, New York, 2017.

generation by worries about whether their own self-portraits on social media will match the self-portraits of their peers, or whether their peers will bother to answer their messages. More deliberate health hazards are videos encouraging self-harm or suicide.

3.9. EXCUSES: FREEDOM OF SPEECH, BRINGING PEOPLE TOGETHER, ONLY A CHANNEL FOR SPEECH OF OTHERS

We have noticed already one of the defences put forward for the funding methodology, that personal data are not shown to the advertiser. But there are others. Mark Zuckerberg has sometimes defended Facebook's practices by saying that free speech requires them. I have argued in chapter 2 that legal prohibition of speech should be exceptional, but that not all speech is good. The case made by John Stuart Mill for the value of free speech, I have pointed out in chapter 2, casts doubt on the value of free speech if it is used in a way that interferes with its benefits. In chapter 1, I found similar benefits presupposed by centuries of Mill's predecessors. I saw the benefits that Mill enumerates as depending on the use of discussion to learn new truths from each other. Our learning the truth, however, is not a central purpose of all social media companies. Search engines can indeed be useful. But if funding depends on promoting advertising or propaganda with too little attention to its source, free speech will privilege most those with deep pockets, and it will not serve the values which Mill was ascribing to free speech of enabling us to learn new insights from each other. According to Sacha Baron Cohen,[46] Mark Zuckerberg has also stated one of his main goals as being to 'uphold as wide a definition of freedom of expression as possible'. This would surely exclude a definition which connected freedom of expression with human benefit. And indeed, according to Baron Cohen, Mark Zuckerberg did not think that Facebook should remove posts denying Hitler's genocide of 6 million Jews between 1941 and 1945. Mark Zuckerberg has also presented it as a central merit of Facebook that it brings people together. But there are now other services that do that, and it needs to be considered whether the *right* people are brought together and the *right* people kept apart. It was mentioned earlier that social media can keep people wrongly apart, dividing them into separate echo chambers on the basis of personal profiles, when they should be together. This is the very opposite of what John Stuart Mill saw as the central benefit of free speech: having people discuss and learn from different viewpoints. But equally, it is not good to put victims together with persecutors or murderers, or propagandists plying disinformation together with the voters they target.

Social media have sometimes supported publication of bad content on the basis of its ability to attract by appeal to Section

46. *The Guardian*, Sacha Baron Cohen, 25 November 2019.

230 of the US Communications Decency Act, which says that a platform is not responsible for the content that passes through it.[47] But Facebook and many other media are not a mere passage for whatever passes through. Facebook deliberately *feeds* its users, as the name *newsfeed* implies, with content, sensational content, and it is said to be willing, in return for payment, to give higher prominence to an item. If so, it cannot disclaim responsibility for the content. Google also arranges content in an order. This is not to deny that for the right purposes an order is desirable.

3.10. THE WIDESPREAD USE OF SOCIAL MEDIA AS A SOURCE OF NEWS VERSUS BETTER FORMS OF PUBLIC PARTICIPATION IN ONLINE NEWSPAPER CONTENT

Given the difficulty of basing reliable news on content designed to attract advertising, it is alarming to read a report from the Pew Center that 62% of US adults get at least some of their news from social media and of these, 64% from just one, most commonly Facebook.[48] More recently, it has been claimed that in

---

47. Frontline's *The Facebook Dilemma*, 25–26 October 2018. Cf. Zuboff, *The Age of Surveillance Capitalism*, pp. 110–112.
48. J. Gottfried and E. Shearer, 'News across social media platforms', Pew Research Center, May 26, 2016, https://www.journalism.org/2016/05/26/news-use-across-social-media-platforms-2016/.

26 countries more than half the population in 2016 were using social media as a source of news, and for more than a quarter of the young in those countries it was the main source of news.[49]

In a much better model, the public was given a very different participatory role by Alan Rusbridger, as described in his inspiring account of creating a version of the *Guardian* newspaper online. Rusbridger agreed with the ideals of journalism as a public service. But he nonetheless thought of that service as compatible with a new involvement of the public. He was not looking for what attracted different members of the public with a view to maximizing profit. Instead, he included selected responses of readers at least on all opinion pieces online.[50] He envisaged using *Guardian* online readers to offer travel tips, Muslim residents to comment on Islamic terrorist attacks, readers from other countries to provide perspective when those countries were discussed, possibly including audience reactions to theatre, as well as the opinions of professional theatre critics.[51] Exposés of alleged events could be assisted by readers from all over the world acting as witnesses with direct local knowledge of them.[52] Moreover, the general public could swiftly return photographic evidence, confirmatory or otherwise, about alleged events by such apps as Instagram or Snapchat, or by audio or video recordings.[53]

---

49. Moore, *Democracy Hacked*, p. 129; cf. pp. 177–178.
50. Alan Rusbridger, *Breaking News*, Canonbooks, Edinburgh, 2018, Chapter 11, 'The future is mutual', especially pp. 106, 113.
51. Ibid., pp. 109–112, 114–115, 230.
52. Ibid., p. 201.
53. Ibid., pp. 153–154.

Rusbridger did acknowledge, however, the problem of abusive, unreliable, or fake contributions. Moderators were not numerous enough to remove all bad reader content, even if the readership might itself help to draw attention to bad content.[54]

3.11. THE TRADITION OF CITIZEN JOURNALISTS

Rusbridger mentioned, but was not keen to use, the term 'citizen journalists', although a practice which might at a stretch be so described goes back, I believe, to the English civil wars of the 1640s. That citizen movement was made possible by the new invention of home printing presses and by women, especially wives, distributing the revolutionaries' pamphlets to thousands, as I have described elsewhere.[55] For the modern use of the terminology, I am grateful to Jane Potter for introducing me to contemporary discussions.[56] The former English revolutionaries were not invited by any editors to publish their pamphlets, but the modern terminology can be applied to non-professional journalists, equally whether they respond to open

---

54. Ibid., pp. 118–119.
55. Sorabji, *Moral Conscience through the Ages*, pp. 138–139, referring to H. N. Brailsford, *The Levellers and the English Revolution*, Cressett Press, London, 1963.
56. https://www.theguardian.com/media/2012/jun/11/rise-of-citizen-journalism https://www.athensjournals.gr/media/2017-3-1-4-Noor.pdf https://www.researchgate.net/publication/332627049_Citizen_Journalism

forums online, or initiate their own content online without prompting.

It can be very important if non-professionals use online facilities to reveal atrocities that governments want to hide, whether by reports, by photography, or by sound recording. Professional journalists cannot be everywhere, but if alerted by non-professionals on the spot, they may be able to reach the right place, in order to make a fuller assessment.

3.12. THE INEFFECTIVENESS OF COMPANY FINES AGAINST MONOPOLY AND MAXIMIZED PROFITS

The monopoly power of the biggest social media is increased by what further organizations they own or work with. Facebook owns WhatsApp and Instagram, Google owns YouTube. There are laws against monopoly, because it suppresses innovative competition. Fines have been imposed, not only for monopoly, but for a variety of the practices discussed. But, once achieved, monopoly, like other methods of maximizing profit, has the further effect of making it affordable to contest or pay fines and hence to continue with unsatisfactory practices.

The European Union in June 2017 imposed a (subsequently contested) fine of 2.4 billion euros on Google for exercising its monopoly.[57] The European Union's Competition

57. *The Guardian*, 28 June 2017.

Commissioner, Margrethe Vestager, announced on 18 July 2018 the imposition of a (subsequently contested) monopoly fine on Google of 4.34 billion euros for pressuring manufacturers to prioritize the Google android phone system over those of any other companies.[58] In May 2017, the European Union fined Facebook US$122 million for 'misleading' statements about Facebook's takeover of WhatsApp.[59] France has also levied a tax on digital monopolies,[60] and in the United Kingdom a former leader of the Labour Party Opposition suggested that the country should levy a monopoly tax on tech firms that stifle competition.[61]

3.13. SWINGING VOTES BY USING PERSONAL PROFILES TO TARGET VOTERS WITH DISINFORMATION IN TWO 2016 VOTING CAMPAIGNS

3.13.1. The 2016 British referendum campaign on whether Britain should exit from the European Union ('Brexit')

A major contribution to the investigation of the UK referendum campaign on 'Brexit' in 2016 was Carole Cadwalldr's publication

---

58. YouTube, 30 July 2018, https://www.youtube.com/watch?v=1–2qxLuWK6g
59. *The Guardian*, Jennifer Rankin, 18 May 2017.
60. *The Telegraph*, 28 December 2018.
61. *The New Statesman*, James Ball, 23 August 2018; *The Guardian*, Editorial, 23 August 2018, https://www.theguardian.com/commentisfree/2018/aug/23/the-guardian-view-on-labours-media-policy-important-contribution-but-more-please

on 18 March 2018, in *The Observer*, re-published online by *The Guardian*. This recorded the confessions of a collaborator, turned whistle-blower, Christopher Wylie, about his own part in targeting voters in the UK referendum campaign about whether Britain should exit from the European Union ('Brexit'). He was mentioned earlier as creating from Facebook's personal data, and with its knowledge, personality profiles of users, expanded by the data of the users' Facebook 'friends'. Wylie now further confessed[62] he had taken part in founding (abroad for safety) a company, Aggregate IQ (AIQ), to target voters on the internet. AIQ was alleged to have exceeded the maximum spending permitted in voting campaigns by having smaller amounts channelled through separate, but coordinated, intermediaries. Wylie said that AIQ managed Cambridge Analytica's technology platform and did the actual targeting of voters on the basis of Cambridge Analytica's data. The man regarded as the chief strategist of Vote Leave, Dominic Cummings, subsequently principal adviser to the British Prime Minister from late 2019, was described as saying, 'Without a doubt, the Vote Leave campaign owes a great deal of its success to the work of Aggregate IQ. We couldn't have done it without them'.[63]

A further allegation about the UK Brexit campaign implicated Russia in funding disguised accounts on Twitter, for paid suppliers of fake news about Brexit and using web robots to multiply the messages. Other internet platforms had not at that

---

62. *The Guardian*, 24 March 2018, Carol Cadwalladr and Mark Townsend.
63. *The Guardian*, 24 March 2018.

time been investigated, but an initial 419 disguised Twitter accounts were identified as coming from Russia, and 45,000 suspect messages about Brexit had come from a number of Twitter accounts created and then removed in the 48 hours just before and just after the Brexit referendum vote.[64]

The role of Russia in UK voting about Brexit caused further anxiety when on 4 November 2019, the chair of the UK Parliament's Intelligence and Security Committee, Dominic Grieve, announced that Prime Minister Boris Johnson had delayed publication of Parliament's official cross-party report on Russian interference in the 2016 referendum on Brexit and in the United Kingdom's 2017 general election. It had been cleared, Grieve said, by security for release and given by 17 October 2019 to Boris Johnson, who had just been elevated by his party to the post of prime minister. But Johnson had earlier led the campaign for Brexit before the 2016 referendum with the erroneous claim painted on his battle bus that the United Kingdom had to pay the European Union £350 million per *week*, which could instead be recouped for the National Health Service. He now delayed publication of the Russian interference report, and on 29 October gained further delay by securing agreement to holding a general election, with a view to confirming his position and policy on Brexit, without voters having seen the report.[65] The delay caused further

---

64. *The Times* (UK), 14 November 2017; *The Guardian*, 16, 17 November 2017, A. J. Vicens, Daisuke Wakabayashi, and Scott Shane.

65. E.g., *The Guardian*, 4 November 2019.

suspicion and sparked a lawsuit from the Bureau of Investigative Journalism.[66] But he won the election, and it remains to be seen when the report will be published.

The UK Information Commissioner, in one of her reports on 11 July 2018, *Democracy Disrupted*, at section 3, explained why her investigation focused not only on social media companies, but also on the *political parties*. It was because it was the political parties that in the United Kingdom commissioned social media for advertising to voters.

3.13.2. *The 2016 US presidential election campaign*

In the 2016 US presidential election campaign of Donald Trump against his rival Hillary Clinton,[67] one Facebook advertisement, targeted on voters revealed to have strongly Christian views, said 'Press 'Like' to help Jesus win'.[68] It showed a white-coloured Jesus Christ supporting Trump opposite the Devil, coloured brown, supporting his rival for the presidency, Hilary Clinton.[69] Voters discovered to be African American and their supporters were targeted with fake news claiming that Hilary

---

66. E.g., *The Guardian*, 14 November 2019.
67. Problems were already exposed in *The Guardian* by Harry Davies on 11 December 2015, in connection with the *earlier* campaign by Ted Cruz in the United States to be nominated as the Republican Party's presidential candidate in the 2016 election, a campaign later won by Donald Trump.
68. Illustrated, in Tamsin Shaw, 'Beware the big five', *New York Review of Books*, 5 April 2015, p. 34.
69. Illustrated, in Tamsin Shaw, 'Beware the big five', p. 34.

Clinton's description, twenty years earlier, of young members of drug gangs as super-predators, was directed against African Americans.[70] It was further falsely claimed that she was receiving money from their enemies, the Ku Klux Klan, a US organization known for murdering African Americans.[71] Another fake slogan, 'The Pope endorses Trump', finished up in Facebook's newsfeed, and it is said[72] that 64% of Americans believed it.

It has been said[73] that in May 2018 Facebook admitted that the firm Cambridge Analytica had accessed 87 million files of data, predominantly from their US users, but including the data of 1 million users in the United Kingdom. Further, according to this account, it had allowed access to users' data to at least 200 apps. And it was said also to be sharing users' data with Apple, Microsoft, Amazon, and nearly 60 other internet device makers, enabling them to download personal data, even when users had denied Facebook permission to share this information with third parties. The data explicitly mentioned here were data on the *behaviour* of users, and it was mentioned that data from tracking the *movements and location* of people can also be traded. Facebook and Google were said also to have embedded

70. Tom Baldwin, *Ctrl Alt Delete*, Hurst, London, 2018, p. 191.
71. *The Guardian*, Jon Swaine, 18 December 2018.
72. *The Guardian*, Jon Henley, 29 January 2020.
73. I take the following information from Sue Halpern, 'The known known', *New York Review of Books* 65.14, 27 September–10 October 2018, pp. 32–38, on pp. 36 and 38.

their advisers in the 2016 presidential election campaign team of Trump, a proposal which Hillary Clinton's rival presidential campaign declined.[74]

The whistleblowing of Wylie, mentioned earlier, on 18 March 2018 proved a new watershed, and the head of Facebook, Mark Zuckerberg, a US citizen, was called, and agreed, to testify personally before the US Congress about the estimated 87 million US citizens whose personal data on Facebook were acquired by Cambridge Analytica for purposes of interfering in the US 2016 presidential election campaign.[75] He testified for nearly five hours on 11 April 2018 before the Senate's Commerce and Judiciary Committees,[76] and the next day for four hours before the Energy and Commerce Committees of the House of Representatives. The House asked about the personal data not of 87 million, as before, but of more than a billion individuals having been extracted by the abuse of phone or email look-up features, and about the ability to acquire personal data about an individual from an individual's *friends* on Facebook, even if that individual did not use Facebook.[77]

74. Moore, *Democracy Hacked*, p. 160.
75. *The Guardian*, Julia Carrie Wong, Sabrina Siddiqui, 27 March 2018.
76. *The Guardian*, David Smith, 11 April 2018.
77. *The Guardian*, Alex Hern, 13 April 2018.

In the week starting 16 December 2018, new reports to the US Senate Intelligence Committee were announced[78] about violations of privacy not previously acknowledged to the Senate. They spoke of the extent of help given by Facebook and other social media to alleged Russian interference with the 2016 US presidential election, and the extent to which Facebook and others had failed to acknowledge this help. Although Russia was said to have used every major social media platform, Facebook was reported to be the most effective at targeting US conservatives and African Americans. It was said that 99% of all uptake on its targeting, in such forms as expressing 'likes' (39 million of them), or implementing 'shares' (31 million) to copy the posts to others, came from twenty Facebook 'pages' controlled from Russia, with names misleadingly implying support for America and for African Americans. Despite the major role of Facebook, its ever-growing subsidiary Instagram was judged in the reports to have gained more impact or 'engagement' and to have contained more nefarious content.

The subsequent reports to the Senate Intelligence Committee claimed that Facebook had revealed to the Senate by April 2018 only some of the Russian posts and accounts, while Twitter and Google submitted their information to the reporters in a form

---

78. *The Washington Post*, 17 December 2018; *The Guardian*, Jon Swain, 18 December 2018; Leader article, 19 December 2018.

very difficult to analyse. This led the senior Democrat on the US Senate Intelligence Committee to say that new laws were needed to tackle a crisis around social media.

3.14. THE EUROPEAN UNION'S DEVELOPMENT OF PRIVACY LAW FOR THE INTERNET AND ITS EFFECT ON THE UNITED KINGDOM AND ELSEWHERE

Although Federal Germany had an early Data Protection Act in 1977, influenced by a 1970 data protection statute in the German province of Hesse,[79] it is the European Union that has recently led the way in developing privacy law in Europe in relation to personal data on the internet. Its 1995 Data Protection directive already led in the United Kingdom to the UK's 1998 Data Protection Act.

In 2014, the European Court of Justice, to which at that time the UK was subject, accepted that some earlier data-retention regulations violated certain principles of *privacy* in the European Charter of Fundamental Human Rights, sections 7 and 8, and new legislation was required of the United Kingdom, which it passed that year. Earlier regulations had not sufficiently required, for example, that retained data be connected to a person who might throw light on crime, or could

---

79. Hartzog and Richards, 'Privacy's constitutional moment and the limits of data protection', (p. 16 of pre-print).

serve the purposes of protecting public security, that there should be rules about who might be allowed to investigate the data and under what procedures, and objective justification for the duration of data retention.[80]

The European Union had already been questioning the privacy rules in the United Kingdom surrounding government retention of the personal data of citizens for security purposes. In 2013, it was revealed by Edward Snowden that in the United States the National Security Agency (NSA) was collecting the phone records of millions of unsuspecting Americans on the basis of secret court orders, and the corresponding British organization (GCHQ, or Government Communications Headquarters) was doing the same with the knowledge of the British Government. In response to a legal challenge initially brought by two British members of Parliament, the European Union's highest court ruled in December 2016 that 'general and indiscriminate retention' of emails and electronic communications by governments was illegal.[81]

The UK's conformity, however, was possibly compromised when in November 2016 it approved a new Investigatory Powers Act, requiring businesses inside and outside the UK to retain

80. Graham Smith and Judith Rauhofer, 'Mandatory data retention legislation lives on in the UK—or does it?', https://uk.practicallaw.thomsonreuters.com/8-577-6488?transitionType=Default&contextData=(sc.Default)&firstPage=true&bhcp=1 Alan Travis, 'Repeal call on day one of "snooper's" law', *The Guardian*, 30 November 2016. I have benefited from a clearer explanation of the European Court of Justice's call for amendments in an unpublished paper kindly shown me by Lord Mance.
81. Alan Rusbridger, *Breaking News*, 2018, pp. 305, 325.

personal data on their customers. It required internet providers to retain for twelve months a record of all websites visited by their users, and phone companies to record information on all calls, and make them accessible to various government agencies, police, and security services. The agencies were given new rights to hack computers and phones, and the cell phones and web records of journalists could, with a judge's agreement, also be inspected. It was laid down that UK data can be accessed also by US security services. But as of 9 September 2017, this Act was reported to have itself been referred to the European Court of Justice to consider its compatibility with European law.[82]

The European Union's new General Data Protection Regulation came into force from 25 May 2018 for all countries in the Union, still then including the United Kingdom.[83] It requires processers who process personal data of residents of the Union, on pain of fines of up to, and in some cases over, 20 million euros, to notify specified controllers about breaches of personal rights within 72 hours of finding them. Internet users may obtain from controllers electronic copies of any data held on them, and confirmation of where and for what purpose it is held. They may ask, with some restrictions, for data to be erased and processing halted,[84] although the implementation of the provision for erasure appears still to have problems,

---

82. Ibid.

83. A preliminary judgement of the European Court of Justice endorsed the decision of Google to respond to requests for data-erasure only within the European Union, *The Guardian*, Owen Bowcott, 11 January 2019.

84. http://www.eugdpr.org/key-changes.html

judging from the experience of Max Schrems, cited previously, whose deletions were immediately replaced. The remedy is in any case limited insofar as the data may already have been copied and used many times before action could be taken. Separate provision is made for personal data on suspected criminals or terrorists to continue being collected and transferred by competent authorities, and this is presupposed in a Directive on Protecting Personal Data for the Purpose of Criminal Law Enforcement, although stronger rules are proposed for protecting the privacy of suspects.

The United Kingdom in the same year, 2018, complied as a member of the European Union, by introducing a new UK Data Protection Act 2018. And similar provisions for data protection may spread further. Canada's corresponding PIPEDA provisions have been deemed adequately compliant with Europe's, but there are proposals for revision to make them fully compliant, adding, for example, the right to having personal data erased.[85] Japan also has an act for the protection of information accepted as adequate by the European Union.[86]

I have had a number of occasions to cite the legal principles of the European Union and the verdicts of its courts as the most helpful for the problems of free speech under discussion. The many European regulations have caused irritation to the

---

85. https://www.westlawnextcanada.com/blog/insider/proposed-changes-to-pipeda-gdpr-ready-for-the-change-969/

86. Hartzog and Richards, 'Privacy's constitutional moment and the limits of data protection' (p. 12 of pre-print), https://papers.ssrn.com/sol3/papers.cfm?abstract_id=3441502

UK government and to many UK citizens. But now, from 2020, the country has departed from the jurisdiction of Europe, and UK citizens risk losing some very important protections in the area of privacy and other rights. Ultimately decisions should not be left to the sole discretion of companies that profit from providing a platform, nor to purely political interests.

Although in March 2017, the founder of the World Wide Web, Tim Berners-Lee, opposed European Union policing, preferring it to be left to the internet companies,[87] by March 2018, after numerous revelations, he called for regulation, legal if necessary, because of the concentration of power locked in to a few platforms, including Facebook, Google and Twitter, and their buying up of other companies.[88]

3.15. RESPONSE IN THE UNITED STATES TO EUROPEAN DATA PROTECTION LAW

In the United States, companies will have to deal with citizens of the European Union in accordance with Europe's law. But in addition, a paper of 2020[89] finds that some of the individual states of the United States are interested in the fair processing of data, even though the federal government is not taking it up.

---

87. https://webfoundation.org/2017/03/web-turns-28-letter/
88. *The Guardian*, Olivia Solon, 'Tim Berners-Lee: We must regulate tech firms to prevent "weaponised" web', 12 March 2018.
89. Hartzog and Richards, 'Privacy's constitutional moment and the limits of data protection', pp. 1 and 21.

The State of California was the first to pass a law expanding consumer privacy rights in 2018.[90] Since then, the paper claims, fourteen more states have introduced, or passed, data protection bills (p. 28), although it warns that in the United States privacy legislation never has the weight of freedom of expression, which is required per an amendment to the US Constitution, whereas privacy can be traded against other interests (p. 46). The sector of commerce in the United States would also welcome data protection for a different reason: the European Union will not share data with countries which it does not judge to have adequate data protection. Some companies have sought to get around this by binding themselves strictly with the US government, or with the US Federal Trade Commission, to abide by the European privacy requirements (pp. 24–25). We shall see in the following that Facebook is also said to be losing some of its popularity with users in the United States, because of fears about privacy.

Despite the absence of US federal privacy law judged adequate by the European Union, the paper draws attention (pp. 15–16) to the influence on other countries of a much earlier US report of 1973 by an advisory committee to the Secretary of the US Department of Health, Education and Welfare. This recommended six 'Fair Information Practices' (or FIPs) in record-keeping systems, following, and possibly influenced by, the UK's Younger Report of 1972 on the handling of information by computers. The principles were

---

90. https://www.dataprotectionreport.com/2018/06/california-passes-major-privacy-legislation-expanding-consumer-privacy-rights/

restated and revised in 1980 in Europe by the Organisation for Economic Cooperation and Development.

3.16. TRUST

The United Kingdom has special safeguards on non-digital political advertisements, which before an election are not allowed on radio or TV, except in rationed election broadcasts permitted to the main political parties at election time. This too, however, is currently upset by the availability of political advertisements on the internet, which has accordingly been questioned.[91] The British Broadcasting Company (BBC) is tightly controlled in its procedures at all times. It is obliged to seek several times a day the best version of the information it is giving.[92] And it is required to represent both sides of a case, where the case is not clear. It is not surprising that in a recent selection of UK news brands, BBC news has the highest level of trust among UK respondents surveyed, for respondents both over and under thirty-five years of age, and the highest level for both left- and centre-leaning respondents, though not for the right-leaning.[93]

---

91. Baldwin, *Ctrl Alt Delete*, pp. 282–283.
92. Ibid., p. 254.
93. Newman, *Reuters Institute for the Study of Journalism Digital News Report 2018, Overview and Key Findings*, p. 11, Why are consumers relying less on Facebook for news?, http://www.digitalnewsreport.org/survey/2018/overview-key-findings-2018/; *Reuters Institute for the Study of Journalism Digital News Report 2018 2.6*, Antonis Kalogeropoulos, 'The rise of messaging apps for news', http://media.digitalnewsreport.org/wp-content/uploads/2018/06/digital-news-report-2018.pdf?x8947

By contrast with the BBC, only 23% say that they trust news on social media.[94] It might be thought that this lack of trust is a safeguard. But lack of trust does not imply disbelief. Rather, lack of trust may leave one wondering which is true and harbouring suspicions equally of the true and the false. That is not a satisfactory situation.

Facebook's *popularity* as a source of news, however, as opposed to its trust rating, remains far ahead of that of the other social media in the Reuters Institute's periodic checks between 2014 and 2018. Nonetheless, popularity can change. WhatsApp, which Facebook bought up, and which, like many other apps, allows restricted circles of users, has been gaining ground. Since 2016, it has risen on both news-charts and any-purpose-charts to second place behind Facebook, and is now 20% behind it. This is still well behind, but what is more interesting is the reasons that people give for discussing news on WhatsApp (owned by Facebook) rather than on Facebook itself. They say:[95] 'I use Facebook less, because I don't want to have a close contact to many of my 'friends' there. These friends on Facebook are not important to me any more. With my inner circle of friends I communicate via WhatsApp'. 'Even though you may disagree with your friend on WhatsApp,

---

94. Newman, *Reuters Institute for the Study of Journalism Digital News Report 2018, Overview and Key Findings*, p. 1, http://www.digitalnewsreport.org/survey/2018/overview-key-findings-2018/

95. *Reuters Institute for the Study of Journalism Digital News Report 2018*, 2.6, Kalogeropoulos, 'The rise of messaging apps for news', http://media.digitalnewsreport.org/wp-content/uploads/2018/06/digital-news-report-2018.pdf?x8947

friends are able to keep that good level of respect, everybody shares their opinion, and anyone who disagrees can joke about it. It's a lighter mood to debate news with friends on WhatsApp than on Facebook'. 'Somehow WhatsApp seems a lot more private, . . . whereas in Facebook for some reason it just feels like it's public. Even if you're in Messenger' (Facebook Messenger is Facebook's own alternative messaging app).

Local Facebook groups are said to have been successful in the election of 2017, so long as local issues remained prominent. But by 15 November 2019, it was reported that younger voters were leaving the group because of extreme views, bullying, and toxicity, believed to be coming in from outside the local area, and preferred Twitter.[96] The report also stated that younger voters were abandoning Facebook often because they were put off by the number of political advertisements.

Facebook is said in a paper of 2019 by John Gramlich[97] to be losing its popularity with some users in the United States because of fears about privacy. He claims that 42% of Americans have taken a break from checking their account for several weeks or more, and 26% have deleted the app from their phone in the past year (roughly 2018).

---

96. *The Guardian*, Aamna Mohdin, 15 November 2019.
97. Hartzog and Richards, 'Privacy's constitutional moment and the limits of data protection', refers (p. 26 of pre-print) to John Gramlich, '10 facts about Americans and Facebook', Pew Research Center, 1 February 2019, https://www.pewresearch.org/fact-tank/2019/02/01/facts-about-americans-and-facebook/

3.17. FACEBOOK'S DECISION-MAKING PROCESSES IN THE TV PROGRAMME *THE FACEBOOK DILEMMA*

On 25–26 October 2018, a new perspective was provided on Facebook's policy-making by the two-part, 100-minute television programme already cited, *The Facebook Dilemma*, which was created by Frontline, an organization funded by charities, many of them devoted to quality journalism. The programme was shown in the United States on Public Service Broadcasting. It was directed by James Jacoby, and it interviewed Facebook executives, including the director, Mark Zuckerberg, as well as former executives who had left, and people who had asked Facebook for particular remedies. It was also briefly reviewed by Sue Halpern, also cited previously, in the *New York Review of Books*, 'Apologise later' (*New York Review of Books* 66.1, 17 January–6 February 2019). That title was taken from a TV shot of Mark Zukerberg saying, 'It's more useful, like, to make things happen and then apologise later'.

There seemed to be a pattern of people alerting Facebook to its being used for wrongdoing, and Facebook doing nothing about it. The programme's interpretation was that the profit motive accounted for reluctance to reduce the use of Facebook, whoever the user.

Among examples offered was the apparent non-compliance with a settlement concerning privacy with the US Federal

Trade Commission.[98] The Defence Department organization DARPA also became concerned about national security implications. But Facebook was said not to have investigated further when it was used by Russian sources for discrediting the Ukrainian government, at the time when it feared a possible Russian invasion of the Ukraine.[99]

As regards the genocide mentioned earlier against Rohingya Muslims in Myanmar, according to the programme, Facebook had received warnings for years from David Madden that it was being used to denigrate the Muslim population in the eyes of the Buddhist majority, for example with caricaturing cartoons and descriptions of them as rapists and terrorists. Despite Madden's warnings, Facebook did not remove any content, and when the homes of the Rohingya Muslims were burnt, many killed, and 150,000 displaced, the United Nations, as already mentioned, said that Facebook had played a significant role in genocide. Sue Halpern's review of the TV programme mentioned Facebook as also being used to support the massacre of Tamils in Sri Lanka.[100]

In Egypt, the programme described Facebook as being used to support the democratic revolution which ousted the ruler Mubarak in 2011, with a young Egyptian Google executive, Wael Ghonim, playing a prominent role. But when the

---

98. David Vladak looked into this; *The Facebook Dilemma*, Part I.
99. Rand Walzman, *The Facebook Dilemma*, Part I.
100. However, so far as I can identify the example from India quoted from the programme by Sue Halpern, it was the murder of only one single person over a dispute on his using an unflattering form of address on a post to a Facebook friend.

counter-revolution took place and restored a different strong man, it equally used Facebook for its victory, and denigrated Wael Ghonim as an Israeli spy. Facebook profited whichever party made use of it.

In the Philippines, the programme reported, President Duterte had a critic of his war against drugs, with extra-judicial killings, Maria Ressa, trolled with hate mail on Facebook through 26 accounts with up to 90 posts an hour, one calling for her death by repeated rape. But Facebook did not, at her request, take down any accounts or intervene, even though it employed her as a fact-checker.[101]

Frontline's programme gave further indications of why Facebook was unlikely to rectify misuses of the sort described, even when it could. Everyone in the company accepted that all decisions would be made by the founder, Mark Zuckerberg, who held the majority of shareholder votes. The advertising model of profitability was revamped in 2008 after consultations by the Chief Operating Officer Sheryl Sandberg. Mark Zuckerberg also continued consulting some colleagues about how best to increase revenue further, as seen in his leaked emails of 2012, mentioned earlier as known to a Parliamentary committee. But as sole decision-maker, he would not presumably have had the salutary constraints of having to seek a consensus or address an alternative viewpoint on revenue. He also did not have to respond to any entreaties. It was a

---

101. A further account of Maria Ressa's case is given in Peter Pomerantsev, *This Is Not Propaganda*, Faber and Faber, London, 2019, pp. 20–33.

long time since Harvard had been able to make him to take a website down.

It is true that he answered very confidently questions put to him by non-experts when he was called before Congress, while the subject was new to them.[102] But he did not normally have to answer experts like Kara Swisher, the woman expert on privacy rights on Frontline's programme. She courteously asked him to explain some of his controversial policies. When that happened, the session was interrupted by his feeling unwell. He said he had had flu, although her subsequent comment was that he seemed to be having a panic attack. Either or both could be true, but what struck me was something different, that he was not used to speaking to an expert courteously asking him to explain to a large audience why he was doing something. Without the ability to explain openly in reply to salutary, but courteous, questions, and the regular practice of this, it does not seem likely that such policies can be properly re-thought. Even the man appointed as head of Privacy, Sandy Parakilas, was shown in the programme as explaining that he left in 2012, because he found that the company had no interest in users' privacy.

To mention one more thing that the programme showed, company apologists were seen all giving similar excuses, as if they had been rehearsed, for the alleged misuses that the programme presented. These problems, it was said, cannot be

---

102. Congress grilled him much more sharply on 24 October 2019.

solved, only contained. The bad can only be minimized. This is no doubt true for some contexts. But it is an inadequate defence for playing a significant role in genocide, or for lending support to major massacres, or for jeopardizing the validity of the democratic electoral system. It is not sufficient to say of such effects that one can only minimize the occurrences.

3.18. OTHER CONTEXTS OF DECISION-MAKING

The access to alternative points of view in decision-making, which Mill thought so important a benefit of free speech, seems also to be curtailed in the Facebook campus at Menlo Park in the San Francisco area. Visitors are not allowed in, unless accompanied the whole time by a friend who works there, and the main workforce is expected to remain on the campus where they have their residence, their transport round campus, a big choice of eating places, and every facility they are expected to want. Indeed, an enthusiastic visitor, 'Heather', accompanied by a friend in 2018 or earlier, described the campus as 'the happiest place in Tech'.[103] But the task set to the workforce, unauthorised capture of electronic data, or 'hacking', was reinforced throughout the site by such names as 'Hacker Way', 'Hacker Square', 'Hacker Company', by stonework spelling out the word 'Hack', and in the

---

103. https://trimmtravels.com/facebook-headquarters-tour/

month of her visit, October had been renamed 'Hacktober'. Of course, hacking is sometimes desirable. We want governments to hack terrorist communications, and we may want others to discover by hacking whether governments or companies are illegitimately hacking our innocent communications without due reason. But the unqualified celebration of hacking might well have deterred members of the Facebook workforce from making proposals on the ethics of hacking. In fact, however, it was reported on 7 November 2019[104] that in late October 2019, hundreds of Facebook employees wrote to Mark Zuckerberg, asking for changes to how the company handled political ads, including limits to the targeting of very small groups.

In this last case, it may turn out that communal participation will have made a difference to final decisions, but the participation does not appear to have been invited.

The lack of communal participation in decisions may have played a role in another context when Mark Zuckerberg did not reply personally to invitations to attend the UK House of Commons Digital, Media and Sport Committee's oral evidence sessions, although that committee did bring together an International Grand Committee from nine other legislatures across the world. Mark Zuckerberg sent representatives to the committee, but it was commented in that committee's Final Report of 14 February 2019, section 30, that the Facebook representatives had not been properly briefed on crucial issues, and did not answer the questions, nor send the answers they had

---

104. *The Guardian*, Alex Hern, 7 November 2019.

promised subsequently. The committee reported that it believed the evasions deliberate. But it may have been that Facebook deliberately left its representatives out of the picture. An engineer representing Facebook before the committee decently admitted that he felt ashamed when hearing of such things as Facebook's refusal to remove posts stirring religious tensions in Sri Lanka.[105] Another representative, when asked why he was selected to represent Facebook, replied that he had merely volunteered.

3.19. REMEDY 1: EDUCATING CHILDREN IN READING SOCIAL MEDIA

There is a positive kind of remedy already in place in a number of countries:[106] the education of children at an early age in how to read social media. Finland is a leading country, because it has had since 2014 to combat fake news from its neighbour, Russia. Finland was placed easily first among 35 European countries in an annual index measuring resistance to fake news. In the Corruption Perceptions Index, 2012–2018, published by Transparency International, Britain came 11th out of 180 countries. But the 2018 Report of the Parliamentary Commission on Fake News and the Teaching of Critical Literary Skills found that only 2% of British children had the skills to spot whether a story was real or fake. But British school

---

105. *The Guardian*, Emma Graham-Harrison, Jim Watson, 27 November 2018.
106. There is a survey of countries in *The Guardian* by Jon Henley, 29 January, 2020.

children who get lessons between ages nine and eleven find the teaching interesting. In teaching programmes based on the UK government's personal, social, health, and economic (PSHE) education programme, they learn to recognize both fake news[107] and targeted news.[108] There is now also a fake news game designed pre-emptively to alert people to, and familiarize them with, the techniques used by others for producing fake news.[109] It is part of the pleasure that nine- to eleven-year-olds take in their pre-emptive lessons that they too practise the techniques as part of the strategy for learning to resist them.

I doubt, however, if this most valuable educative development could ever protect *everyone* from fake news and targeting. If not, it is unfortunately necessary to consider also the difficult and less agreeable question of how non-compliant social media might be controlled.

3.20. REMEDY 2: COUNTER-MESSAGING OF HATE AND TERRORISM SPEECH ONLINE AND PREDICTION OF CONCENTRATIONS

For hate speech, an organization called Moonshot has invited the interest of hate messagers by advertising online with such

107. https://www.theguardian.com/newswise/2019/oct/07/lesson-5-spotting-fake-news-pshe-education
108. https://www.theguardian.com/newswise/2019/oct/07/lesson-6-understanding-that-news-is-targeted-pshe
109. https://www.aboutbadnews.com

notices as 'Join ISIS' or 'Bomb manuals' and has used trained workers, including former extremists, to offer psychological redirection, including the option of chatting.[110] Another organization, HateLab, has measured the times and places towards which online hate and terrorism speech is concentrated, without identifying individual authors of messages, in order to prepare authorities against violence or terrorism.

3.21. REMEDY 3: NEW LEGISLATION ON DETAILS AND ON A GENERAL DUTY OF CARE

I have already mentioned some areas in which new legislation may be needed about fuller revelation to users and to appropriate judicial authorities of how personal data are being collected and used. It was argued that Facebook does not as yet reveal enough to users about how their profiles are constructed.

In addition, legislation would be needed to require social media companies, if asked by suitable judicial authorities, to identify advertisers who have paid them for illegal advertisements that target groups matching certain profiles and the individuals to whom they have sent such advertisements. In the United Kingdom, the Information Commissioner's Office is already using statutory powers to seek such information. But

---

110. For my information here, I have drawn on Simon Parkin, 'Trigger Warning', *The Guardian Weekend* magazine, 2 May 2020.

social media companies should be under an obligation to supply it to such bodies.

The buyers of illegal advertisements, as well as the sellers, should be made legally liable, especially in cases to which the UK Information Commissioner drew attention, in which a political party or agent buys from the social media the targeting of deceptive messages on voters, in order to swing an election. In these cases, it is the political parties or agents who initiate the manipulation.

Messages of hate or intimidation sent to victims on social media not by the media themselves, but by agents making use of the media, are not so easy for the media to detect and remove. But legislation can at least require social media to show that they have taken reasonable measures for their detection and removal. This is where a legal duty of care comes in, as described in the Berggruen Institute's report, *Renewing Democracy in the Digital Age*.[111] Such a law does not attempt to specify unlawful content. Focusing instead on *harm*, it is easier to implement and harder to evade. The UK government has proposed, and many of its committees have endorsed, a statutory requirement for social media providers to take reasonable steps to prevent people coming to reasonably foreseeable harm from the operation of their services. It also requires the providers to appoint

111. Berggruen Institute report, *Renewing Democracy in the Digital Age*, March 9, 2020, 'Rebuilding the public square in the digital age', pp. 16–21, with Appendix B, pp. 31–32; William Perrin, 'Implementing a duty of social care for internet platforms', https://www.berggruen.org/ideas/articles/renewing-democracy-in-the-digital-age/

a regulator. The regulator was to be bound to observe people's rights by the European Convention on Human Rights and was to be paid by a mixture of government funds and levy on the companies.

As regards political interference with voting campaigns, the recommendations of UK watchdogs also need to be given effect. The Information Commission, the watchdog with most powers, set up by Act of Parliament as early as 1998, and sponsored by the House of Commons Digital, Media, Culture and Sport committee, was wise to put pressure on political parties as well as private companies, when protecting electoral procedures, for reasons given earlier. It not only made requirements of political parties, but also arranged to audit their compliance by a named date. Its powers also enabled it to collect substantial records of electoral and other practice by electioneering firms. It can itself issue fines for breaking the law, although at some point it needs to ask the courts of justice to enforce the law.

Another relevant commission, the Electoral Commission, has been starved of powers, and has had to ask Parliament for more. The UK Government needs to address this and bring legislation before Parliament for strengthening it, but so far appears not to have acted.

We saw that the recommendations of the Information Commission's Investigation Update were affirmed in the Final Report of the UK House of Commons Digital (etc.) Committee, but both await response from the Executive, that is, from the Prime Minister and senior ministers who form the Cabinet, all from the ruling party in Parliament. Until they respond, it will not be known what changes in law the Executive might submit to Parliament. The minister for Digital (etc.) has made some comments, but ministers are often moved from their current posts, so it is still unclear what legislation, if any, can be expected.

In France, by contrast, in preparation for the 2019 elections to the Parliament of the European Union, President Macron proposed the creation of a 'European Agency for the Protection of Democracies', which would offer the services of experts to individual member states seeking to protect their elections. He also proposed banning foreign financing of European political parties.

In all these cases, Government has a large role to play, but good proposals will not necessarily turn into law without further support. A central claim of Shoshana Zuboff's *The Age of Surveillance Capitalism* is that in some Western countries a campaign of ordinary people is needed to press government into action. There cannot be such a campaign if people do not know the somewhat secretive ways of some social media companies.

3.22. THE NEED FOR ENFORCEMENT

Legislators also need to consider carefully how to *enforce* legislation on those trading in personal profiles in ways which have once been made illegal, whether selling or buying targeted advertisements. As regards selling, compliant social media should be positively encouraged. We have seen, on the other hand, that *fines*, however large, do not deter companies which are themselves large enough to contest or pay the fines.

The same would be true of *compensation* for damages sought in lawsuits. But there is in any case no possible compensation for genocide, or for jeopardizing the democratic electoral system. Recommendations were made in the *Online Harms White Paper* introduced by the UK government in April 2019, with a view to eventual legislation. In section 6, *Enforcement*, at 6.5, it was proposed that there should be liability not only of companies, but also *personal liability of individual members of senior management* in social media for civil fines or even criminal liability. This could make it hard for non-compliant companies to recruit executives. The burdens of personal liability are bound to be felt, in a way that company liability may not be. Individuals are not in the position of companies which can afford to pay or contest fines indefinitely, and companies may find it harder to cover the costs of their executives as well as their own. Individuals are also less likely to be willing to evade the law by moving to countries that have not ratified the legislation, because they would not be able to return with impunity. However, there is more than one solution to this particular problem of companies booking their profits into countries with a low tax rate.[112] The *White Paper* referred to personal liability,

112. In 6.9, the White Paper further recommended that in the case of companies without a legal presence in the UK, where international collaboration failed to secure conformity to law, a last resort would be blocking platforms from being accessible in the UK. A different proposal has been endorsed by the OECD (as reported in the Berggruen Institute report, *Renewing Democracy in the Digital Age*, March 9, 2020, https://www.berggruen.org/ideas/articles/renewing-democracy-in-the-digital-age/, p. 33, of collecting tax in countries where internet giants actually make, not technically book, their money.

already introduced into Financial Services. My attention has also been drawn to personal liability recently introduced into the scandal concerning the alleged concealment of diesel emissions from Volkswagen cars,[113] and in the case of top executives of Barclays Bank allegedly concealing a payment from Qatar to investors.[114] Even in the United States, the Consumer Data Protection Act introduced to Congress by Senator Ron Wyden seeks to hold executives personally liable for certain lapses in automated decision systems, although this Act is not thought likely to be passed.[115]

3.23. A BETTER WAY

In a talk I gave, based on this chapter, on 28 October 2019, I said, 'How much better it would be if the leaders of some social media companies powerful enough to influence others voluntarily initiated a reform of practice themselves'. The next day a rival company, Twitter, announced that it would no longer host political advertisements.[116] This sounded at least a welcome concession, albeit modest, assuming Twitter would still host

---

113. Karin Matussek and Christoph Rerwald in *Bloomberg*, 24 September 2019, and Jasper Jolly et al. in *The Guardian*, Monday, 30 September 2019, a case brought to my attention by Reinholdt Munzberg.
114. BBC News, 9 October 2019, a case brought to my attention by Orde Levinson.
115. Hartzog and Richards, 'Privacy's constitutional moment and the limits of data protection' (pre-print p. 32).
116. *The Guardian*, Julia Carrie Wong, 30 October 2019.

personal tweets from politicians. But the same day, by contrast, Facebook went on to announce that it *would* continue political advertisements. Twitter elaborated[117] that it would ban all electoral candidates, elected officials, and political parties from advertising, but allow some not-for-profit organizations to promote messages about social issues. This at least attempted the difficult task of trying to distinguish between different types of communication, as opposed to repeating a single phrase like 'free speech'. Twitter's decision also appeared to be prudent, judging from the report mentioned earlier,[118] that younger voters were abandoning Facebook often because they were put off by the number of political advertisements. This may provide support for the prediction made to me eleven days earlier by a younger participant in an academic discussion that some people might prefer paying a subscription to seeing so many political advertisements.

Reforms were announced also by Google, which said that from February 2020, it would limit advertisers' access to personal data, to stop advertisers associating individual users with such categories as religion, politics, and sexual orientation. By 21 November 2019, Google had worked out a sample of further distinctions. It would ban doctored images and videos, misleading claims about census records, and demonstrably false claims that could undermine trust in elections or the

---

117. *The Guardian*, Julia Carrie Wong, 22 November 2019.
118. *The Guardian*, Aamna Mohdin, 15 November 2019.

democratic process. Political advertisements that refer to election candidates, political parties, or measures that were the subject of a current ballot would be allowed to target voters only through the use of data about their age, gender, or address, not of more sensitive data. The new restrictions would apply to the UK general election called for December 2019 and to the US presidential election of 2020.

There are, however, other areas in which reform is needed. *The Financial Times* had an article on 15 November 2019[119] about reaction to its discovery that some of the UK's most popular websites, including Google, were sharing sensitive data such as medical symptoms and diagnoses with companies.

3.24. THE CONTINUING NEED TO CONTROL POLITICAL PARTIES

Unfortunately, there was confirmation of the UK Information Commissioner's earlier stress on the need to control the use of social media *by political parties*. As reported by *The Financial Times*,[120] in the campaign for the UK general election held on 12 December 2019, the currently governing UK party (it is not

---

119. *The Financial Times*, Madhumita Murgia and Alex Barker, 15 November 2019, 'Google plan to lock down user data draws fire from advertisers'.
120. *The Financial Times*, Jemima Kelly and Sebastian Payne, 21 November 2019.

said whether this was the Prime Minister's office) was able to get around some of the reforms of Twitter and Google for securing electoral honesty. Google would still be able to prevent the party repeating its earlier electoral trick of doctoring a video, to make it appear that a leading member of the opposition had been unable to answer a certain political question. But at election time, according to the *Financial Times* report, the governing party had misleadingly rebranded its account on Twitter as an independent fact-checking service. This could enable it to evade Twitter's ban on political advertisements, and it also put the party's interest in retaining power ahead of one of our few safeguards against the misuse of social media: our ability to rely on the trustworthiness of fact-checks.

The governing party was also said to have gone on to buy a deceptive web address, www.labourmanifesto.co.uk, in order to present a fake election manifesto implied to be that of the leading opposition party. Moreover, it was said to have used funding to make the fake manifesto (properly labelled by Google as an advertisement) appear automatically as the top search result for any user of Google who sought 'Labour', on the day that the Labour Party published its actual election manifesto.

The two hired individuals named as running the governing party's digital strategy for the UK general election were said to be New Zealanders, so foreign to the UK, and to have already operated, as foreigners in Australia, a strategy which helped to produce an unexpected victory in the last Australian general election. The two New Zealanders would have been working in the UK under another Australian, Isaac Levido, the head of the governing party's election strategy, and formerly the right-hand man of the Australian election strategist mentioned previously, Lynton Crosby. It looks as if foreign election agents can be hired who are not, under existing law, legally responsible for their actions in the country whose elections they influence.

3.25. RETROSPECT

Freedom of speech and expression is an essential value. When it needs to be restrained, I have in the first two chapters recommended *voluntary* self-restraint and voluntary thought about good ways to open ears. The *law* is difficult to frame and can be difficult to implement. But in this chapter, turning to those social media whose funding methods threaten the basic freedoms of their users, and politicians who exploit this, I think that, not only new education, but also new legislation is necessary to sharpen up the distinction between legitimate and illegitimate practices. There needs to be increased public awareness, to allow for leading executives of social media and their individual supervisors, and also individual politicians, to be held personally liable for violation of the law.

APPENDIX

Protecting privacy: The slow development of privacy law

In contrast with the European Union's General Data Protection Regulation, privacy law had hitherto been slow to develop. But the new social media funding based on personal data has made privacy an urgent issue. The right to privacy was recognized in the United States by Samuel Warren and Louis Brandeis in 1890,[121] and was treated by them as falling under the right to be let alone, a paraphrase of the Fourth Amendment of the US Constitution: the right of the people to be secure in their persons, houses, papers, and effects, against unreasonable searches and seizures. Some laws protecting privacy are more directly connected with freedom of speech than others, because they are concerned with *publicising to others* claims about a person's private life, rather than with intruding on it in a more direct way. In the United States, there is a common law tort of unreasonable *disclosure*, as well as of unreasonable *intrusion*. But Robert C. Post has argued that both torts have limited effect.[122] Restrictions on publicising can once again run against

---

121. 'The right to privacy', *Harvard Law Review*, vol. 4, 1890, pp. 193–220. I again thank Dan Robinson.
122. Robert C. Post, 'The Social Foundations of Privacy: Community and Self in the Common Law Tort', *California Law Review* 77, 1989, pp. 957–1010, Yale Law Faculty Scholarship Series, Paper 211.

the free speech basis of First Amendment jurisprudence in the United States. But in particular Post raised doubts about treating as matters of legitimate public concern the private lives of 'voluntary' public figures, for example celebrities. Does telling about their private lives contribute to the kind of public debate needed for a democratic nation? The question is even more pressing about the private lives of non-public figures.

About English common law, Stephen Sedley has said[123] that it included no law of privacy in 1765 other than the law of trespass, and that there was still no privacy law as such in 1990, but only a law protecting one's confidential information, which sometimes had to be forced into use as a substitute. But things began to change through European influence, on the basis of the European Convention on Human Rights first passed in 1953, including its Article 8.1 on privacy. This protected private life, family life, home, and correspondence, which later came to include emails. At the European Court of Human Rights, Princess Caroline of Monaco got a ruling in 2004, against paparazzi photographers, that the public had no legitimate interest in her public life, unless it was required by public debate in a democracy. If passed earlier, this might have saved the life of Princess Diana in the United Kingdom, who

---

123. Stephen Sedley, 'Sex, libels and video-surveillance', Blackstone Lecture, Oxford, 2006, printed in *London Review of Books*, repr. in *Ashes and Sparks*, Cambridge University Press, Cambridge, 2011, pp. 311–324.

died when she was chased by paparazzi in 1997. It was also the kind of decision that Robert Post looked for in vain in the US courts, that merely being a public figure was not enough. Thus again, there has been a divergence between the US courts and European courts, which up to 2019 at least included the United Kingdom.

BIBLIOGRAPHY

Amar, Akhil Reed. 'The creation and reconstruction of the First Amendment',
Ch. 3 in Daniel N. Robinson and Richard N. Williams, eds., *Religious
Liberty, Essays on First Amendment Law*, Cambridge University Press,
Cambridge, 2016, pp. 36–63.

Antognazza, Maria Rosa. 'Leibniz's doctrine of toleration, philosophical,
theological and pragmatic reasons', in J. Parkin and T. Stanton, eds.,
Natural Law and Toleration in the Early Enlightenment, Proceedings of
the British Academy, 186, Oxford University Press, Oxford, 2013, pp.
139–164.

Antognazza, Maria Rosa. 'Truth and toleration in early modern thought',
in Richard Whatmore and Ian Hunter, eds., *Natural Law and Politics*,
Cambridge University Press, Cambridge, 2019.

Bajpai, Rochana. *Debating Difference: Group Rights and Liberal Democracy in
India*, Oxford University Press, New Delhi, 2011.

Baldwin, Tom. *Ctrl Alt Delete*, Hurst, London, 2018.

Baltussen, Han, and Peter J. Davis, eds. *The Art of Veiled Speech*, University of
Pennsylvania Press, Philadelphia, 2015.

Bejan, Teresa M. *Mere Civility*, Harvard University Press, Cambridge, MA, 2017.

Berggruen Institute, *Renewing Democracy in the Digital Age* report, March 2020.

Bhargava, Rajeev. 'Beyond toleration: Civility and principled coexistence in Asokan edicts', in Alfred Stepan and Charles Taylor, eds., *Boundaries of Toleration*, Columbia University Press, New York, 2014, pp. 173–202.

Bhatia, Gautam. *Offend, Shock, or Disturb*, Oxford University Press, Delhi, 2016.

Brown, Peter. *Power and Persuasion in Late Antiquity*, University of Wisconsin Press, Madison, 1992, pp. 61–70.

Chafee, Zechariah, Jr. *Free Speech in the United States*, Harvard University Press, Cambridge, MA, 1942.

Chandrachud, Abhinav. *Republic of Rhetoric: Free Speech and the Constitution of India*, Penguin Random House, Gurgaon, India, 2017.

Cohen-Almagor, Raphael. 'J.S. Mill's boundaries of freedom of expression: A critique', *Philosophy* 92, 2017, pp. 565–596.

Erskine, Thomas. verbatim record of Speech in Defence of Thomas Paine, 1792, included in *The genuine Trial of Thomas Paine for a libel contained in the second part of Rights of Man; at Guildhall,* London, December18, 1792, 2nd edition 1793.

Feinberg, Joel. *Offense to Others*, Oxford University Press, Oxford, 1985.

Fish, Stanley. 'The dance of theory', in Lee C. Bollinger and Geoffrey R. Stone, eds., *Eternally Vigilant: Free Speech in the Modern Era*, University of Chicago Press, Chicago, 2002.

Fiss, Owen M. *The Irony of Free Speech*, Harvard University Press, Cambridge, MA, 1996.

Foucault, Michel. *Fearless Speech*, Semiotext(e), Los Angeles, 2001, ed. Joseph Pearson from lectures at Berkeley, October–November 1983.

Gandhi, Mahatma. 'Is this humanity?', 1926, seven lectures in Mahadev Desai, in his *Day to Day with Gandhi*, vol. 8, Varanasi, 1973.

Garton Ash, Timothy. *The File*, Random House, New York, 1997.

Grant, Edward. 'The condemnation of 1277: God's absolute power and physical thought in the later Middle Ages', *Viator* 10, 1979, pp. 211–244, repr. in his *Studies in Medieval Science and Natural Philosophy*, London, 1981.

Halevi, Ilan. 'Vers une guerre des civilisations? L'affaire des caricatures du Prophète', in *Du souvenir, du mensonge et de l'oubli. Chroniques palestiniennes*, Éditions Actes Sud, Paris, 2016, pp. 227–241.

Halpern, Sue. 'Apologize later', *New York Review of Books* 66.1, 17 January–6 February 2019.

Halpern, Sue. 'The known known', *New York Review of Books* 65.14, September 27–10 October 2018, pp. 32–38.

Hartzog, Woodrow, and Neil Richards. 'Privacy's constitutional moment and the limits of data protection', *Boston College Law Review* 61, 2020. pp. 1–79.

House of Commons Digital, Culture, Media and Sport Committee, Final Report 2019, Disinformation and 'fake news' Index on Censorship 45.1, Spring 2016, *Staging Shakespearean Dissent.*

Information Commissioner's Office, UK, *Investigation into the Use of Data Analytics in Political Campaigns*, 11 July 2018.

Konstan, David. '*Parrhēsia*: Ancient philosophy in opposition', in Albert A. Anderson, Steven V. Hicks, and Lech Witkovski, eds., *Mythos and Logos*, Rodopi, Amsterdam, 2004.

Konstan, David. 'Two faces of *parrhēsia*: Free speech and self-expression in ancient Greece', *Antichthon* 46, 2012, pp. 1–13.

Mill, John Stuart. *On Liberty*, 1859.

Moore, Martin. *Democracy Hacked*, One World, London, 2018.

Neier, Aryeh. *Defending my Enemy*, Dutton, New York, 1979.

Newman, Nic. *Reuters Institute for the Study of Journalism Digital News Report 2018*, 2.5, 'Donations and Crowdfunding: an emerging opportunity?'

O'Neill, Onora. *A Question of Trust*, The BBC Reith Lectures 2002, Cambridge University Press, Cambridge, 2002.

O'Neill, Onora. *Speech Rights and Speech Wrongs*, Van Gorcum, Amsterdam, 2016.

O'Neill, Onora. 'Trust and accountability in a digital age', *Philosophy* 95, 2020, pp. 3–17.

Philodemus. *On Frank Criticism*, with Greek and translation by David Konstan, Diskin Clay, Clarence E. Glad, Johan C. Thorn, and James Ware, Scholars Press, Atlanta, GA, 1988.

Pomerantsev, Peter. *This Is Not Propaganda*, Faber and Faber, London, 2019.

Post, Robert C. 'Religion and freedom of speech: Portraits of Muhammad', *Constellations* 14, 2007, pp. 72–90, repr. in Andráa Sajó, *Censorial Sensitivities*, Eleven International, Utrecht, 2007.

Post, Robert C. 'The Social Foundations of Privacy: Community and Self in the Common Law Tort', *California Law Review* 77, 1989, pp. 957–1010, Yale Law Faculty Scholarship Series, Paper 211.

Robinson, Daniel N., and Richard N. Williams, eds. *Religious Liberty, Essays on First Amendment Law*, Cambridge University Press, Cambridge, 2016.

Rusbridger, Alan. *Breaking News*, Canongate, Edinburgh, 2018.

Sandel, Michael. *Democracy's Discontent*, Harvard University Press, Cambridge, MA, 1996.

Scanlon, T. M., Jr. 'Freedom of expression and categories of expression', *University of Pittsburg Law Review* 40, 1979, pp. 519–550.

Sedley, Stephen. 'Sex, libels and video-surveillance', Blackstone Lecture, Oxford, 2006, printed in *London Review of Books*, repr. in *Ashes and Sparks*, Cambridge University Press, Cambridge, 2011, pp. 311–324.

Shaw, Tamsin. 'Beware the big five', *New York Review of Books*, 5 April, 2015, p. 34ff.

Sommerstein, Alan H. 'Harassing the Satirist: The alleged attempts to prosecute Aristophanes', in I. Sluiter and R. M. Rosen, eds., *Free Speech in Classical Antiquity*, Mnemosyne Supplement 254, Brill, Leiden, 2004, pp. 145–174.

Sorabji, Richard. 'The cross-cultural spread of Greek philosophy (and Indian moral tales) to 6th century Persian and Syriac', *Studia Graeco-Arabica* 2019, pp. 147–163.

Taplin, Jonathan. *Move Fast and Break Things*, Little Brown, New York, 2017.

Thapar, Romila. *Aśoka and the Decline of the Mauryas*, Oxford University Press, Delhi, paperback edition, 1998.

Thijssen, J. M. M. H. *Censure and Heresy at the University of Paris, 1200–1400*, University of Pennsylvania Press, Philadelphia, 1998.

Thijssen, J. M. M. H. 'Condemnation of 1277', *Stanford Encyclopaedia of Philosophy*, http://plato.stanford.edu/entries/condemnation/ (with bibliography).

Truschke, Audrey. *Culture of Encounters: Sanskrit at the Mughal Court*, Columbia University Press, New York, and Penguin India, New Delhi, 2016.

Twenge, Jean M. *iGen*, Simon and Schuster, New York, 2017.

Warburton, Nigel. *Free Speech: A Very Short Introduction*, Oxford University Press, Oxford, 2009.

Weisberg, Jacob. 'The autocracy app', *New York Review of Books* 65.16, 25 October–7 November 2018.

Zuboff, Soshana. *The Age of Surveillance Capitalism*, Profile Books, London, 2019.

INDEX

For the benefit of digital users, indexed terms that span two pages (e.g., 52–53) may, on occasion, appear on only one of those pages.